How to Run for Political Office and Win

EVERYTHING YOU NEED TO KNOW TO GET ELECTED

Melanie Williamson

HOW TO RUN FOR POLITICAL OFFICE AND WIN: EVERYTHING YOU NEED TO KNOW TO GET ELECTED

Library of Congress Cataloging-in-Publication Data

Williamson, Melanie, 1981-
  How to run for political office and win : everything you need to know to get elected / by Melanie Williamson.
      p. cm.
  Includes bibliographical references and index.
  ISBN-13: 978-1-60138-408-9 (alk. paper)
  ISBN-10: 1-60138-408-4
  1. Campaign management--United States--Handbooks, manuals, etc. 2. Political campaigns--United States--Handbooks, manuals, etc. 3. Campaign management--United States--Case studies. 4. Political campaigns--United States--Case studies. I. Title.
  JK2281.W55 2011
  324.70973--dc22
                              2011011678

Printed in the United States

Printed on Recycled Paper

PROJECT MANAGER: Melissa Peterson
INTERIOR LAYOUT: Antoinette D'Amore • addesign@videotron.ca
PROOFREADER: Andrell Bower • bowera@gmail.com
FRONT/BACK COVER DESIGN: Jackie Miller • millerjackiej@gmail.com

A few years back we lost our beloved pet dog Bear, who was not only our best and dearest friend but also the "Vice President of Sunshine" here at Atlantic Publishing. He did not receive a salary but worked tirelessly 24 hours a day to please his parents.

Bear was a rescue dog who turned around and showered myself, my wife, Sherri, his grandparents Jean, Bob, and Nancy, and every person and animal he met (well, maybe not rabbits) with friendship and love. He made a lot of people smile every day.

We wanted you to know a portion of the profits of this book will be donated in Bear's memory to local animal shelters, parks, conservation organizations, and other individuals and nonprofit organizations in need of assistance.

– *Douglas & Sherri Brown*

PS: We have since adopted two more rescue dogs: first Scout, and the following year, Ginger. They were both mixed golden retrievers who needed a home.

Want to help animals and the world? Here are a dozen easy suggestions you and your family can implement today:

- *Adopt and rescue a pet from a local shelter.*
- *Support local and no-kill animal shelters.*
- *Plant a tree to honor someone you love.*
- *Be a developer — put up some birdhouses.*
- *Buy live, potted Christmas trees and replant them.*
- *Make sure you spend time with your animals each day.*
- *Save natural resources by recycling and buying recycled products.*
- *Drink tap water, or filter your own water at home.*
- *Whenever possible, limit your use of or do not use pesticides.*
- *If you eat seafood, make sustainable choices.*
- *Support your local farmers market.*
- *Get outside. Visit a park, volunteer, walk your dog, or ride your bike.*

Five years ago, Atlantic Publishing signed the Green Press Initiative. These guidelines promote environmentally friendly practices, such as using recycled stock and vegetable-based inks, avoiding waste, choosing energy-efficient resources, and promoting a no-pulping policy. We now use 100-percent recycled stock on all our books. The results: in one year, switching to post-consumer recycled stock saved 24 mature trees, 5,000 gallons of water, the equivalent of the total energy used for one home in a year, and the equivalent of the greenhouse gases from one car driven for a year.

Dedication

· ·

This book is dedicated to the friends and family who have helped me through the process of writing.

Table of Contents

Introduction

. . . .

Although state and national elections gain the most coverage and receive a higher voter turnout, local governments affect our lives the most. Local governments are responsible for the streets we drive on, the water we drink, and the police and fire protection we depend on for our immediate safety. Local governments oversee schools and after-school programs. Although the conditions of the state and federal economies affect the local economy, a lot can be done at the local level to help promote business. Local governments also affect the atmosphere of the community through planning and supporting local events, such as city festivals and entertainment. Local governments also deal with local taxes, infrastructure, safety, and environmental issues.

Federal and state political leaders often begin their careers in local politics. It provides them with the experience needed to move forward. Although politicians at the federal level are involved with major decisions concerning issues such as trade, foreign relations, and war, local politicians make decisions every day that affect the people with which they live and work.

If your political dream is to influence people's lives, help your neighbors, and make an impact on your community, serving in a local political office is the best move you can make. However, serving in a local political office requires an individual who cares for the community and its well-being.

Often, people who serve in local office are trying to give back to the communities they live in. Locally minded individuals have the interest of their home area first in their heart. They will work hard to meet the needs of their particular area. They see the potential of the area they want to serve and feel they can help achieve its goals. They have ties in the community whether they have lived there their whole lives. Local office is a hands-on type of government in which, compared to someone in a state or national office, you are readily accessible to your constituents.

Depending on the size of the municipality, local political officials might be considered full- or part-time employees. Their time commitment can range from working a few hours a week to being on call 24 hours a day for seven days a week. Before you run for the position, know whether a political office is full or part time. Although most people think of mayors and council members when thinking of local offices, the public elects a variety of positions ranging from clerks and sheriffs to judges and coroners.

Deciding to run for one of these positions is just the first step in the journey to becoming an elected local politician. This book was created to help you examine the steps necessary to run for local office and, more importantly, to win.

The term "local politician" refers to politicians at the city, township, village, and county levels. The term "mayor" can refer to the mayor of Sheffield Lake, Ohio, with a population of about 9,000, and the mayor of New York City, with a population of more than 8,000,000. The information provided in this book is meant to address campaigns and elections of all sizes.

This book will delve into the different types of local political offices and the types of local government different areas of the country have. Looking at state and national government, you will learn how these types of offices compare. For those with political dreams beyond the local level, the book discusses which offices best lead to positions at the state and national level.

The book will look at the role political parties have in local elections and discuss what the terms Democrat, Republican, Conservative, and Liberal mean and how none of the terms are synonymous. You will learn about the role of primary elections in areas in which one party dominates. When to run can be a major consideration, so the book will help you weigh your options and tell you what to look for when going up against an incumbent.

You need to follow many technical steps when running for any political office, and the book will enumerate the legal requirements, including filling out paperwork and disclosing certain information to the public, most elected officials face when deciding to run.

Your campaign structure is another important consideration that includes mobilizing your support, talking to constituents, and gathering information about the issues that affect the community in which you intend to hold office.

Politics is all about building connections, and the book discusses how to reach out to your supporters and those already in local office. Developing these relationships in the early stages of campaigning can be a way to show voters you are ready to lead.

You will learn the benefits and pitfalls of hiring professionals to manage your campaign and your message. We will look at the roles of public relations specialists, campaign managers, and other professionals you might want to consider.

No campaign can exist without money, and fundraising is one of the most important tasks any politician can undertake. The book discusses fundraising and the use of public and private funds in your campaign.

In addition to money, you need to know who your opponent is and what his or her message is. The book discusses the role of debates, town hall meetings, and public appearances. Along with that, it will examine the darker sides of campaigning, including mudslinging and character attacks. Whether your campaign will use these tactics will ultimately fall on you, the candidate. For many, it is a moral and ethical question. This book will help you look at the benefits and pitfalls of using such tactics and how to make the best decision for the type of election you are running in. The book looks at the role political action committees (PACs) can play in local elections.

Although mudslinging and other shady tactics might be age-old practices, the use of technology in elections is a relatively new and growing phenomenon. Social networking, e-mails, websites, and blogs can reach a lot of voters and save you advertising and promotional dollars.

The book looks at the days leading up to the election and discuses last-minute campaigning tactics. In addition, the book discusses how to read polls and election results and how to interact with your opponent. Your campaign is a long journey, but what you do on election day can be just as important as everything else you have done. What you do after the campaign might be just as important as what you do during the actual race. After reading this book, you will learn how to respond to the election results with grace no matter the outcome.

You have won — now what? Campaigning does not end just because the election is over. Find out what you need to do to get ready for your re-election campaign and how your term in office will be a big factor in the next election.

But what if the results are in, and they are not in your favor? Not every campaign has a happy ending, but even a loss can be turned into future success. Learn how to capitalize on a loss by learning from your mistakes and emerging even stronger in the next election.

Whatever the result, getting involved in your local government is a rewarding journey and can open your eyes to the issues facing your area. By giving your time, energy, and passion to serving in a local office, you can shape the future of your county, city, or town and make it a better place to live.

CHAPTER 1

Types of Political Office

Before you decide to run for government office, you should first understand the different types of political positions you can hold. The type of government your local area operates under will determine the available elected positions. Investigate the type of government and its possible positions in your area to decide whether any of the available positions coincide with your personal aspirations and political goals. Whether a town, village, city, county, or district government, local municipalities have many options from which to choose. However, choose wisely because choosing a position that does not suit your skills and experience could cost you the election.

Getting Started

As you learned in school, the U.S. political system divvies up the powers of government among three levels. At the top level is the federal government; second is the state government followed by the local government. Each level has its own powers, limitations, and responsibilities. Officials elected at each level of government can only work within their specific powers. However, they must be aware of what is happening in other levels of government to best serve their office.

Each level is also broken down into smaller categories. The categories are numerous at the local level because of the many different types of local government. Local governments are broken up into a county, or parish if you live in Louisiana; city; village; or town. Outside that hierarchy is the school district, which often acts independently from the other types of government and can sometimes stretch over several political boundaries. Depending on the area, the city, parish, township, village, or county might run the school system. The following table provides a brief overview of the different levels of government and the common political offices within each level. The list of political offices is not an all-inclusive list because there are so many possible variations at the state and local level.

LEVEL OF GOVERNMENT	ELECTED POSITIONS
Federal	President and Vice President
	Representative to the House of Representatives
	Senator

LEVEL OF GOVERNMENT	ELECTED POSITIONS
State	Governor
	Representative to the state's House of Representatives
	State Senator
	State Coroner
	Attorney General
	Secretary of State
	Director of Public Instruction
Local	County officials
	City, parish, village, or township officials
	School district officials

State and Federal Government

Most state governments are set up to mimic the federal government with a single executive and a legislative body composed of two houses, although there are exceptions. For example, at the state level, many elected positions are similar to those at the city and county levels. Many states choose to elect their attorney general, secretary of state, or director of public instruction. Many states also have an elected state coroner. This is something to remember when running for local office if your ambitions are to reach a higher office.

At the federal level, fewer elected positions are available because the Senate is made up of 100 members, House of Representatives has 435 members, and there are only one president and vice president. If serving in a federal political office is an aspiration, the best place to start is local politics. Serving at any level of local government will give you the experience required to run for a state or federal position. By learning how to work within political systems and honing your campaigning skills at a local level, you can hope to give yourself an edge at the state and federal level that leads to success both during and after the election.

Local Government

The different types of local government are a result of population or geographic factors. Each type has a different relationship with the constituents it serves. The following sections offer a look at the different types of local government from what is the smallest in terms of population up to the type of government that generally covers the largest population.

Town government

Town governments govern the smallest number of people. For most states, towns are rural areas that are a step below a village. Villages are more densely populated but are a step below even more densely populated cities. However, in some states, such as Massachusetts, the town government ranks above the village government and below the city.

For most states, the town is a sparsely populated area with about 800 to 2,500 constituents. Some towns have as many as 10,000 to 20,000 citizens, yet the responsibilities of the elected officials of the town are similar. Most towns are set up with a board of supervisors that is proportionate in size to the number of citizens it represents. Depending on the population of the town, town boards have as few as three supervisors or as many as ten.

The board of supervisors oversees the town government's responsibilities, including maintenance of streets and roads. More densely populated towns can sometimes provide their constituents with fire and police services, sanitation services, and other services often associated with a village or city. More often, town governments will partner with a nearby village or the county to provide those services.

In addition to the town board of supervisors, the town will also have an elected clerk and an elected board of assessors to determine property disputes. The clerk's role is to keep track of records, place newspaper announcements of upcoming meetings and law changes, keep track of meeting notes, and provide the supervisors with the resources necessary to make good decisions.

Town supervisors and clerks often are not full-time positions. With a sparse population, few towns have issues that cannot be resolved within one or two monthly town meetings. Still, getting elected and staying in office as a town supervisor will require the candidate to reach out to constituents and work hard. With such a small population to govern, many town supervisors and clerks are well-known in the communities they serve and are directly accessible to the constituents they govern.

Village government

Not all states have villages, and not all villages have a government separate from the city or town in which they are located. Some states have villages in name only; they are not a separate entity. States that recognize villages as a government entity vary in their definition of a village, but most are based on population. In some states, the definition of a village varies from county to county. States that recognize villages use the government structure described below.

A village is also a small community similar to a town, but it is more densely populated and must manage more responsibilities to its constituents. Because there are additional responsibilities, the village government requires more public servants than the town government. Villages are made up of an elected village president and village board. The village will also elect a clerk; a board of public works; a planning commission; and depending on the size of the village, a board of public protection, which governs the police and fire services.

Villages are sometimes tasked with providing and maintaining streets; fire and police protection; sanitation; and public utilities, including water. The village government also often oversees parks and recreation and library services. Unlike towns, villages are often made up of larger village boards, and the president runs village meetings. The village president can either be elected by the village at large or elected by the village board to run meetings. Village presidents are different than mayors in that they have no veto power and are a member of the village board. Some village presidents, however, might not have a vote on the board, and their role is to preside over meetings, facilitate discussions, and break any tied votes.

Village board members or trustees also serve on various committees the board as a whole assigns and might meet several times a month as a committee or as a board to complete the business of the municipality. Despite the added workload, most village trustees are still only part-time employees of the village.

The village clerk, however, is often a full-time position. The village clerk oversees the day-to-day operations of the village, including collecting paperwork, such as building permits and taxes; managing the payroll for city employees; and maintaining the records of the village government. These tasks are much more time-intensive and require someone to be present at the village hall during regular working hours to meet with constituents and collect the paperwork. In addition to working full days, they might have to work some nights. Village clerks also keep meeting records at public hearings and make sure all meeting notices and minutes are properly published according to local laws.

City government

City governments generally govern a large densely populated area and have responsibilities beyond those of elected individuals in towns and villages. Due to this increase, city governments can be complicated and require many elected officials to run effectively. There are three types of city governments a municipality can use: mayor and council, council and administrator, and council and council president. However, it is important to note that due to the differences in size and population, some cities use a combination of the city government organizations described in the following sections. For example, a city might have both a mayor and a city manager.

Mayor and city council

The most common type of city government is the mayor and council form. In this setup, an elected mayor and an elected city council run the city similar to the state and federal models. The executive, often the mayor, has certain powers and responsibilities, and the council has other specific powers and responsibilities. Each branch of the local government is accountable to the other to provide a balance of power similar to the one set up in the U.S. Constitution in which each branch of government has checks and balances over the other branches.

Just like the federal model, the city model's balance of power is meant to keep one group from passing laws that favor only a certain group of individuals. In this model, the mayor's office can make sure a law or statute benefits the city. The city council also has the same power to oversee the actions of the mayor to make sure he or she is acting in the best interest of the city.

The role of the mayor can differ depending on how it was set up in the city charter. The city charter is the document filed with the state that requests city status for a municipality and lays out the details for the type of government the city will have and its boundaries and services it will provide. Most mayors have the power to propose changes to a city's laws; appoint city officials, including the police chief, public works director, and other officials; and propose a budget.

The council oversees many of the law-making responsibilities, approves or denies mayoral appointees, and works with citizens and the mayor to provide the necessary guidance to help complete the day-to-day business of the city. The council also oversees the police and fire departments and public works departments; ensures streets and sidewalks are safe and passable; and manages the staff at city hall, including the city clerk, public works director, and all other city administration.

Depending on the size of the city, the mayor might be a full-time position. Smaller cities, such as Mooringsport, Louisiana, which has a population of 804, will have part-time mayors. In a city with a small population, a full-time mayor might be an inefficient choice because the workload will likely not be enough to fill an entire day. For large cities, a position on the city council can be a full-time position, but for most cities, these politicians only work part time. They will still meet at least twice a month as a group and often having additional committee meetings from which they bring recommendations to the council as a whole.

Council administrator and common council

The council administrator model is another popular model for city government. In this model, the elected common council appoints a city administrator to perform the day-to-day tasks of running the city. Because the administrator is not an elected official, the administrator is accountable to the council and cannot appoint officials. That job now rests with the common council. The city administrator, also known as a city manager, is just that. They manage city operations, review employee performance, and make decisions based on city laws and council directives.

The downside of this type of government is voters do not have direct input into the executive branch of the local government, and the person in the administrator position has no check on the city council. The upside is the administrator is responsible to the council, which might be more in line with the wishes of all the citizens than would be a mayor who a little more than half the population of a city elected. This could mean the administrator considers more opinions when making decisions.

Council president and common council

Similar to the council and administrator form of government, this model also does not include a mayor. Although every common council will elect a president to run meetings, appoint members to committees, and be the spokesperson for the group, the council and council president model takes that one step further. In this model, the council president acts like a mayor but within the confines of being a member of the common council. The council president can appoint officials, propose a budget, and perform other duties similar to a mayor or administrator.

This model of city government is not widely used due to its obvious downfalls. Because the common council rather than the population at large elects the council president, only the constituents in the president's district elected the person acting as mayor. The council president might have at heart the interests of those in the district or ward from which he or she was elected over the entire city because a majority of the voters in the city did not elect him or her. Still, this type of government can be used in a smaller city in which it would not be financially feasible to have a separate mayor or hire a city administrator.

Other types of elected city positions

Depending on the size of the city, elected individuals fill several other positions in city government to perform various tasks, including managing city money, managing the paperwork, or dispensing justice. The amount of compensation and whether these positions are full or part time varies based on the size of the city. The responsibilities of each position might also vary slightly. Know the specifics for the position in your area before deciding to run for office.

City clerks

City clerks perform many of the same duties as their town and village counterparts. Also like towns and village clerks, city clerks are full-time employees. City clerks collect permits, handle the paperwork related to the day-to-day operations of the city, and generally work with other elected and nonelected city employees. The city clerk is also responsible for ensuring all political candidates are following election laws.

City treasurer or comptroller

For many large cities, handling the money that flows through the city is a job a dedicated position needs to do. This is the role of a city treasurer or comptroller. For smaller cities, this role can be included in the responsibilities of the city clerk position, but larger cities need this position. Someone running for this position should have a background in accounting.

City judge

City judges hold trials for matters that include violations of city ordinances. For some cities, having a full-time city judge does not make sense because of the small number of cases. Those cities might choose to appoint a part-time or traveling judge who will hear cases once a month. The traveling judge can also partner with the county to have cases heard in the county court. For larger cities with a bigger workload, an elected city judge is more common. Obviously, a judge should have a working knowledge of the law and the role of a judge, but someone wishing to be elected as a city judge should also have an extensive knowledge of the laws within the specific city in which he or she plans to serve.

County government

As the chapter has moved through the levels of local government, the complexity of each form has grown with the population and land area of a municipality. This will remain true for county government, which is the largest type of local government. It also has the most responsibility out of the different forms of local government. Counties oversee a large area with many people and have the responsibilities of collecting and distributing tax revenues to the different municipalities under its jurisdiction; registering land ownership; and providing emergency services, jails, recreational and park services, health services. To accomplish these tasks, county governments are made up of many individuals — elected and appointed. But across the country, the elected body that oversees county government comes in different sizes.

County board

The county board model of government is the most popular form of county government. The board provides the oversight and legislative duties for the entire county. Supervisors elected from the districts in the county as state and local law determine make up the board. The county board elects a president to preside over the meetings, but the board as a whole makes all appointments and decisions.

In this form of county government, each area of the county is evenly represented, but it can also lead to large and unruly county government bodies, which require the different elected supervisors to build relationships within the board to get key measures passed. In larger counties, the county supervisor can be a full-time position, but in most cases, supervisors are part time.

County commissioners

Another popular form of county government is the county commissioner model. The commissioner model is a smaller form of government that leads to greater accountability but requires full-time commissioners to run the day-to-day operations of the county. The county commissioner model often features three to five commissioners the county as a whole elects. These commissioners wield quite a bit of power over all aspects of the county government, including elected and nonelected officials.

County commissioners set budgets, appoint nonelected officials, and pass laws. Because of the size of the county commissioner system, their accountability to voters keeps commissioners in check. In a county board system, supervisors can hide an unpopular stance behind a large number of votes from the large body.

The size of a county commissioner system lets each constituent know how the commissioner voted.

County executive and county board

Counties with a large metropolitan area or that provide many services to many people might employ an executive and board model of government. Like the mayor and council model, the county executive and county board model mirrors the federal government. This allows for a well-monitored division of power and responsibility.

The county executive serves as the executive branch of the county government by overseeing employees, appointing nonelected officials, and proposing laws and budgets. The council serves as the legislative body by passing laws and approving or denying appointees and proposals. The county executive is often a full-time position and has many responsibilities within the county structure. The county board can also be full time in some bigger counties.

Other elected county positions

In addition to the board and executive, several other offices at the county level are elected positions. To be completed effectively, some of these offices call for special skills, which you should take into consideration when deciding whether to run for a county office.

County clerk

Clerks are a recurring theme in local government. Any level of government will require a lot of paperwork and skilled individuals to maintain and organize those documents effectively. At the county level, the government deals with more people and multiple municipalities under its jurisdiction. Clerks do not take on some of the responsibilities, such as treasurer, assessor, and tax collector, you might see a town, village, or city clerk undertake.

That is not to say the job of a county clerk is less difficult than the jobs of clerks in smaller areas; it is much more difficult. County clerks often must have a staff to deal with the amount of work that goes through their offices. Dealing with such a large area and population demands the county clerk be more specialized in his or her job and leave tax collection, payroll, and other tasks to other departments.

County treasurer

In most states, counties are the main entity taxing property. These taxes are what fund town, village, city, school, and county governments. The county, however, is tasked with collecting these taxes and parceling them out to the different municipalities because counties cover a large area that includes these other municipalities. To have the county act as a single collection point for taxes makes the taxpayers' lives easier because they do not have to send checks to multiple government offices to pay their property taxes each year.

The county treasurer oversees this tax collection, and his or her office distributes the money. Like the county clerk, the county treasurer oversees a staff, and his or her office is highly specialized due to the nature of the work. The county treasurer should be trained in accounting and have a solid working knowledge of financial issues and tax laws so he or she knows how to properly apply the law and understands its effects. However, treasurers without this background have been elected before. In addition to tax collection, the treasurer's office can help create the county budget in a county executive model or be charged with creating the budget in a county board style of government.

County sheriff

The county level is the only level of local government with an elected sheriff. The practice of electing a county sheriff is widely practiced across the United States. The county sheriff is the highest form of police authority in the county. In the early years of the country, simply giving that job to a person was perhaps not thought to be a good idea. Because the sheriff must be accountable to the voters, the sheriff should have at heart the interests of the people rather than the politicians who hired him or her.

A county sheriff is responsible for patrolling county roads, providing law enforcement to towns or villages that might not have their own police force, and upholding the peace in the county. The county sheriff's department also runs the county jail and makes arrangements for housing and transporting prisoners. The sheriff's department is also responsible for providing security and bailiffs for the county judges and overseeing the county deputies.

County judge

City judges are primarily tasked with upholding city ordinances. Similarly, offenders who break state and county laws or commit felonies are brought before the county judge. The county judge is elected and is a full-time position. Some counties might employ multiple judges to account for larger workloads. Judges can be high-profile positions because the court cases they handle can sometimes end up in the media. Consequently, constituents might become familiar with a certain judge's name. Elections for judges favor those versed in law, including lawyers and those who have served as city judges.

County attorney

The county attorney tries cases on behalf of the county in fiscal and legal matters in which the county is involved. The county attorney also counsels the members of the county board on how to run meetings and resolve issues according to the law. A county attorney is not similar to a district attorney who the state employs to prosecute criminals. County attorneys might at times represent the county against individuals in cases of property tax or child care payment disputes, but they do not try criminal cases.

Constable

Though the constable position might be rolled into the sheriff's responsibilities in some areas, some counties still have separately elected constables, who are also known as peace officers. The constable's duties are to enforce codes and ordinances that are not of a criminal matter and hand out citations for violations of those laws. Those ordinances can include building permits, environmental violations, or other property disputes. They also might be called upon to deliver warrants or serve court notices. Although the duties of a constable vary from state to state and county to county, the constable position generally is less dependent on a strong law background and could be a good way for someone without law experience to gain experience for a run at the sheriff's position.

Coroner

The county coroner's duties are to maintain and issue death certificates, determine cause of death, and identify any suspicious deaths for the sheriff's department. The working environment of a coroner could be one of the downsides of the position. Coroners are called on to determine that a person is deceased at a crime scene and sometimes deal with gruesome or unpleasant scenes. The coroner could also be responsible for contacting the next of kin of a deceased individual. The legal qualifications to be a coroner vary by area, so check with the local government to find out how to qualify to be a coroner.

County assessor

The county assessor determines the value of property in the county. The assessor works closely with the treasurer's office to determine the tax bill for the different parcels in the county. The county assessor keeps the records of property ownership in the county and tracks improvements that have been made to the land. The county assessor's position is vital to the county because all revenue comes from property taxes, which the county assessor helps generate. A good candidate for the assessor position would be someone with knowledge of land and home values and with a background in surveying.

Table 2: Elected positions at the city and county levels

CITY-LEVEL ELECTED POSITIONS	COUNTY-LEVEL ELECTED POSITIONS
Mayor	County board members
Council members	County commissioners
City clerks	County clerk
City treasurer	County treasurer
City judge	County sheriff
	County judge
	County attorney
	Constable
	Coroner
	County assessor

IN THE HEADLINES

The role of local governments and their importance in the election process came to the forefront in 2000 as the nation watched a legal battle unfolding in Florida that would ultimately decide who would be the president of the United States. Former Gov. George W. Bush and former Vice President Al Gore were locked in a close contest the state of Florida finally decided. However, a month after the ballots were cast a winner was finally declared. Afterward, the role of local governments in the election process would be put on trial in the U.S. Supreme Court.

Local municipalities are responsible for creating, counting, and certifying ballots for all elections. County and city clerks work together to get the ballots printed with the names of those eligible and running for the contested office. Furthermore, as would come to the forefront in Florida, the clerk's office is responsible for determining in which manner people will vote. Votes are cast in many ways this country. One way is through voting machines with which a lever is pulled to choose the candidate you want. Another more popular way to vote is with punch ballots. However, in Florida, this style of voting led to much legal wrangling and eventually raised questions about standardizing the way the country votes.

As the election night wore on, Florida was quickly identified as a key battleground state. A battleground state is a state in which pre-election polling shows neither candidate has an insurmountable advantage. The fates of the candidates went back and forth in the course of that night. The state was called for Gore early in the vote-counting process and then later for Bush as more tallies came in. As the night turned into the early hours of the next day, the state was officially undecided and left as one of the few states to be undeclared for either candidate. Bush was later named the winner, but the two candidates' vote counts were within 1,000 votes, which, by state law, triggered an automatic recount. Some counties subsequently reported errors and misleading ballots that might have led to voter confusion.

The ballots the county or city clerks had created came under scrutiny, but this was not all the clerks had on their minds. As candidates postured for the best possible outcomes, some manual recounts were requested. A manual recount requires that someone hand count each vote by studying the ballot to see which candidate the voter intended to vote for. The manual recount could drastically change any results because the human eye can pick up more information than the automatic counting machines. Some of the biggest problems were punch cards that were merely dimpled, or not completely punched through, which left what came to be known as "hanging chads." Punch cards were not the only culprits because circles that were not completely colored in also presented recounters with problems.

With an enormous number of votes to count by hand, the task fell to the local governments and, more often, to the clerk's office and the election boards. Coordinating volunteers and securing the ballots in this highly charged atmosphere was a difficult task, and court motions started and stopped many recounting efforts. In the end, the U.S. Supreme Court settled the matter. The event shed light on the role local governments play in the election process and gave city and county clerks another reminder of why their role in the election process is so important.

School Boards

Although county government might be one of the most complex forms of government because of its size, another large body of government is easy to understand. School boards generally govern a large area with a large population, but the creation of school districts is relatively simple. Some school boards only control the schools within one specific city while some school boards combine smaller cities that cannot support a school system on their own. For example, the Sheffield-Sheffield Lake City Schools school board in Ohio controls one school system that services the families of Sheffield, Sheffield Lake, and Sheffield Village. Primarily in rural areas, county school boards control the school system for an entire county.

Because the scope of what school districts do is narrow, the only elected body of the school district is the school board, which is made up of members from the different municipalities within the district. The school board sets policies, approves contracts, and hires and works with the superintendent of schools and the administrative staff.

The school board's duties include setting educational policy for the school administration to follow and give oversight to make sure those policies are carried out. They also set a budget for the district and determine curriculum. Like most legislative bodies, school boards do not require a candidate to have any special skills to run for the position.

CASE STUDY:
ADVICE FROM A
SCHOOL BOARD MEMBER

Leslie Jacobs
Board of Education

I was interested in running for common council; however, I was strongly encouraged to run for the school board. I gained support because I was well educated and because I did not have children. People saw that as a sign that I was not running with ulterior motives.

The campaign itself was not overly challenging. I funded the campaign through successful fundraising efforts. I was already familiar with the election laws, so I did not have to do any additional research. I focused my campaign on the positive attributes I had to offer. I do not believe negative campaigns are fair or necessary. For getting the votes, I believe name recognition is the best thing any candidate can obtain. This can be accomplished through mailings and visiting voters at their home.

Deciding Which Office is Right for You

Now you have looked at the different possible political offices at the local level, take this information and apply it to the area in which you live. Get a better idea of whether you want to run and in which position you are interested. The following checklist will walk you through this process. Making the decision to run for a political office is only the first in several important decisions you will need to make on the path to political office.

☑ CHAPTER CHECKLIST

- ❑ Find out the type of local government under which your area operates.

- ❑ Get a list of the elected positions from the clerk's office.

- ❑ Research each position to determine the qualifications needed to be successful in the position.

- ❑ Disregard any position for which you are not qualified.

- ❑ Research the responsibilities of the remaining positions to determine whether they fit your qualifications.

- ❑ Talk to people who formerly held the position to determine the time commitment involved.

- ❑ Based on this information, decide whether you want to run for a particular political office.

CHAPTER 2

Starting on Your Path to an Election Win

n Chapter 1, you learned about the different possible positions within local government, and you have decided whether running for a particular political office is right for you. Now you need to make some additional important decisions. First, you need to decide whether you should run for a political position. There is a big difference between wanting to do something and deciding it is the right thing to do. You need to determine why you want to run for office and what your political goals are going to be. You should also determine whether you have a chance of winning or whether the process will be a waste of time and money. To determine this, you need to take a careful look at the constituency, your possible support, and who you will potentially be running against. You also need to determine the role politics will play in the election and how you can work it to your advantage. For example, some areas are staunchly Democrat or Republican. Running as a candidate for the opposing party will be an uphill battle from the start. This is not to say you should not run; it is just something you need to be aware of and ready to deal with during the campaign.

Should I Run for Political Office?

The following are some questions you should ask yourself when deciding whether to run for political office:

- **Which position do I want to run for?** There are many types of local political positions. Finding the right one for your goals and schedule is important to being a successful candidate. After completing the checklist at the end of Chapter 1, you should have a better picture of the position you plan to run for.

- **How much time do I have to campaign?** Running for political office takes time and effort. Deciding how much time you want to put into a campaign can help you determine whether running for a political office is right for you. *This will be discussed extensively in Chapter 5.* You also need to decide how much personal money you want to invest in an election.

- **What are your political goals?** Different offices play different roles in deciding policy. Knowing what you want to accomplish as an elected official can help you decide which office you want to run for. What are the political goals of the people you will represent? Your goals should match the goals of the people you will represent.

- **Is there a need for change?** Getting a handle on what the constituents in your area want out of their government is key. Running against a popular incumbent might not be a good idea when first trying to break into politics.

CASE STUDY:
MAKING THE DECISION
TO RUN

Carol Hess
http://politicalresources.com
chess@politicalresources.com

Seeking public office can be an exciting and rewarding experience. It can also play havoc with your personal and professional life. If you are considering running for elected office, you should take consider the following questions. Answering these tough questions will give you a better perspective on many of the elements involved in making that decision.

1. The big question is: Why do you want to run for office?

  a. Do you have a desire for or interest in public service?
  b. Do you have strong feelings on a number of key issues?
  c. Do you feel leadership needs to change?
  d. Do you think you can do a better job than the incumbent?
  e. Can you answer the question of why you want to run for office in one sentence?

2. Do you have a strong sense of your own worth and believe in yourself?
3. Can you ask friends, family, and associates for money and other assistance?
4. Can you withstand criticism and have your personal life closely scrutinized?

5. How does your family feel about you running for office? Are they 150 percent behind you?
6. What will happen to your job while you run? Can you put in the amount of time necessary to win?
7. Can you face the thought of being defeated?
8. Have you thought carefully about the amount of stress, expense, and exhaustion that are part of political campaigns?

Take a moment and evaluate yourself.
1. Do you like people?
2. Are you personable?
3. Do you like meeting people?
4. Do you speak well in public?
5. Can you respond quickly and analyze a situation under pressure?
6. Can you handle frustration?
7. Are you in good health?

If you answered "yes" to the above questions, you are ready to think about the next step in running for office. Campaigns take skill and commitment. There is some luck, but mostly, it is hard work.

Which Political Position Do You Want?

The biggest factor in deciding whether a political position is right for you is whether you have the time to take on its responsibilities. As discussed in Chapter 1, some political offices can be part-time positions that allow for busy individuals to take part in local government while still having a separate career. On the other hand, a local government position can also be a full-time job.

Many of these full-time jobs might not pay as much as a professional job in the private sector, and this must play into your decision. How much time are you willing to give to the political office you are running for? How much time are you willing to give to campaigning for that office? How much money do you need to maintain your current lifestyle? Are you willing to cut that lifestyle back if your position in office will not support it?

Campaigning for an office is a difficult, time consuming process that sometimes can take up to 40 hours per week and might not run on a flexible schedule. Does your work schedule allow you to campaign effectively for four to six months, which is the length of many campaigns? Voters will remember well a candidate who does not show up to a debate or public appearance no matter what his or her political leanings are.

Another factor in running for political office is family concerns. Although local offices do not carry the high-profile lifestyle a state or national position might carry, there still can be stress on family members. Are family members excited about your decision? How much time can you devote away from your family responsibilities? Answering these questions will help you decide between running for a position that is demanding on your time or one you can devote less time to and test the waters with. For those just starting out, the best move might be to run for a less demanding office until you get a feel for the political system.

Setting Your Political Goals

Some positions can help lead candidates to higher offices in the state and federal government. Now is a good time to set your political goals. To do so, answer the following questions:

- What is your reason for wanting to serve the public?

- Who are you aiming to help?

- What are your long-term goals?

Many individuals give years of service at the local level and never have ambitions to run for positions above the local level. For those people, possible reasons for wanting to run might be to effect change in their towns or cities, make the towns or cities better places to live, or help their neighbors live better lives. For those individuals, careers as local politicians certainly have the potential to fulfill their goals. By staying in the local arena, they are able to effect more instant and lasting change for those they care about, including family and friends. If you lean toward this feeling, finding the right office that you can stay in at the local level is a good place to start. If you have a skill set that lends itself to a particular local office, you can use that to gain leverage for an election and might be successful in accomplishing your goals.

For those whose ambitions might reside at the state or federal levels, beginning your political career locally can help you achieve those dreams. Holding any office can only help a candidate's chances of being elected to a higher office down the road. The experience one gets when serving in a public office translates to all levels of government. However, if making a Senate run or being elected as governor is your goal, you might want to tailor your early political experiences to work toward those goals. Being elected and serving on a city council or county board is a good start for a candidate who wants to be a legislator in the future. By serving on a county board or city council, you get a taste for the legislative process and learn to work with others effectively. It also gives you experience you can point to when running for the higher office. For someone who wants to be governor, a stint as mayor or county executive might be a good place to start because officials in these positions perform executive functions similar to those a state governor performs.

In both of these examples, because the local government body mirrors the state and federal body so closely, the candidate is gaining valuable experience in those specific areas. However, no matter your ambitions, there is no bad place to start. What's more, those ambitions might change over time as you become involved in local government. Someone who wanted to progress to a higher level of government might find he or she is happy at the local level. Conversely, someone who thought he or she would want to stay at the local level might suddenly decide he or she wants to be a part of more sweeping changes. The point of choosing an office based on political goals is simply to help you narrow your options and make you think about a potential plan of attack should you decide to run. This will help keep you from wasting time on offices and positions that do not suit your interests.

For those with ambitions for higher office, another way to choose which political office to run for is by working with a local political party. Local political parties sometimes look to gain support for their candidates and eventually get their policies in place by supporting certain local offices. For example, a political party might endorse a city's mayor if it believes that endorsement will lead to the mayor supporting the party's choice for a county position. By working with the political party, you can run for the office it suggests and show you are willing to work with the party to help it reach its goals. This can set you up for an office in a higher level of government when it becomes open. If you have a track record with the party, it might back you when you run for a seat in the state or federal government because it knows you will represent its views. Aligning yourself with a political party early in your political career can be both beneficial and detrimental. You need to take a look at the political climate of your area before you make this decision because some areas of the country are strongly in one camp or the other.

Even if your ambitions are to eventually run for higher offices, do the best possible job at the local level. If the people you are serving feel you are using them as a stepping stone, you will not get much local support in future elections. Additionally, understanding the needs of the community you serve and aligning your goals to their goals is the best way to be successful. Candidates who go into office with their own personal agenda despite the needs of their constituents rarely do well long term.

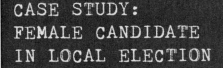

CASE STUDY: FEMALE CANDIDATE IN LOCAL ELECTION

Jeanna Mastrodicasa
City of Gainesville
University of Florida
Commissioner At-Large, Assistant Vice
President for Student Affairs
mastrodij@cityofgainesville.org

Even though she has been interested in politics since she was a little girl, Jeanna Mastrodicasa never dreamed she would run for political office one day. In high school, she helped a city council member run for office in her hometown. As a college student, she interned at the Georgia General Assembly.

In 1997, Mastrodicasa moved to Gainesville, Florida, in pursuit of an advising position at the University of Florida (UF). Her involvement at the university deepened when she became assistant dean of students in 1999, associate director of the honors program in 2000, and finally the assistant vice president for student affairs.

In the early 2000s, she joined the Democratic Executive Committee and restarted the Young Democrats Club at UF. Mastrodicasa assisted several local campaigns, and her peers encouraged her to run for office.

In July 2005, Mastrodicasa filed to run for the seat of City Commissioner At-Large for Gainesville. She ran on a platform of environmental stewardship, public safety, decreased costs, and stronger neighborhoods and was elected to office in March 2006 for a three-year term. She was re-elected in March 2009 for a second three-year term.

Mastrodicasa said her life at the moment is all about balance. She starts her day at the university, makes her way to city hall for appointments and meetings in the afternoon, and then concludes her day back at the university. "It's a lot of back and forth, but it's very scheduled," Mastrodicasa said.

In a standard week, she works about 32 hours at the University of Florida and 8 hours at city hall. She receives 80 percent of her salary from the university and makes about $30,000 a year as commissioner. "If you can live on that, more power to you, but you have to have a plan for financial survival if this is going to be your full-time job," she said.

Before running for office, Mastrodicasa participated in three campaign training sessions. She first attended EMILY's List Training Program for pro-choice women candidates. In 2004, she attended a session with Democracy for America. She also participated in a training session for women candidates that covered small but significant details, such as how to properly sit in a chair when wearing a skirt.

She recommends female candidates attend training courses because of the scrutiny women often face when running for a political position. During her race, she was surprised to see a series of comments about her appearance on a political blog.

Personal attacks seem to be unavoidable when the competition and stress of a political race intensify. She remembers the words of her campaign manager during her first campaign. "He told me always be positive, you never go negative. That is the last resort. You never do it, because negative campaigning does not work," she said. Mastrodicasa said the negative candidate has never won in any Gainesville race.

After Mastrodicasa filed to run for office, she received several e-mails from eager students at the University of Florida who requested to be volunteers for the campaign. A team of about five volunteers was created to help raise money and activate the community for her candidacy. She delegated tasks and was thankful for a graduate student's experience with data management.

She recommends using voter information from past elections to target voters. She said one of her volunteers would run the data from past elections and determine where to knock on doors and solicit votes for the campaign based on the information.

"You can pull the list from the supervisor of elections office, and it shows you exactly who votes and how many times. That's the key information," she said.

Identifying the opinion leaders in the community and those who seldom vote is helpful when determining where to focus campaign efforts. Mastrodicasa said in local races, it is important to reach out to voters, interest them in the campaign, and make sure they get to the polls. She has witnessed many candidates waste money on nontargeted advertising. She said if candidates disseminate messages without a strategy, they might target people who do not vote and do not care or who are ineligible to vote because they do not live in the district or city of candidacy.

"We pulled a data set of all of the UF faculty and staff who live in the city limits of Gainesville and put together a mailer with a group photo of faculty and staff who supported me," she said. She attributes direct, targeted mailers to the success of her campaign in 2006.

Throughout the nine months of Mastrodicasa's campaign, direct mail consumed the majority of her budget. The commissioner also created a Facebook page to gather support and developed a website with PayPal to collect electronic donations. "(PayPal) definitely helped, but it wasn't the majority of donations. It was a means to get donations quickly at the last minute," the commissioner said. She would send out e-mail blasts when she was short on funds and collect immediate donations through PayPal to sustain the campaign.

The commissioner also obtained financial support from fundraising parties at neighbors' homes and from knocking on doors. "Every weekend, (of both elections), I did knock on doors and introduce myself and say, 'Hi. I'm Jeanna Mastrodicasa, and I would like to ask for your support,'" she said. "It's hard to do, but you can't bail when you're the candidate. You have to do it. You have to be willing to put yourself out there."

Furthermore, she distributed yard signs and magnetic bumper stickers. The commissioner warned that many candidates waste money buying "fluff" such as pens, magnets, and signs. "You really need to be talking to the voters and connecting with them by mail or knocking on doors," she said. "You can get all the stuff in the world with your name on it. It does not matter."

During her 2009 campaign, there was an unpleasant referendum issue regarding gender identity that affected her campaign significantly. "I was up for re-election, and I had voted yes to adding the gender identity issue. All four of my opponents were for removing it," Mastrodicasa said. At city forums, those who opposed the amendment harassed her. "There were a lot of issues clouding the campaign," she said.

Throughout the nine-month campaign, the commissioner said she looked normal and unruffled compared to her competition. The forums provided the public a glimpse of the possible future leadership of Gainesville. Mastrodicasa said candidates should look at the key issues, be positive, and be confident. She said if the candidate is intimidated by the process or uninformed about the issues, it shows.

"The best advice I can give is to work on somebody else's campaign and learn how to do it. It's really a process, and every community is a little different, so work on a campaign or two, volunteer, help out," she said.

The commissioner said it takes time to meet the opinion leaders of the city and understand the community. "Get that experience before you jump in and run," she said. Mastrodicasa advises those interested in running for a political office to be patient and informed on issues in the community and neighborhoods that make up the city. "Running a campaign is exciting and fun, but there are a lot of steps in the middle that people don't see," she said.

For more information about Commissioner At-Large Jeanna Mastrodicasa of Gainesville, Florida, please visit the City of Gainesville's website at **www.cityofgainesville.org**.

Gauging Your Future Constituents

Once you have decided to run, measuring the political climate of your area might help you grapple with the question of which office to run for. This entails several criteria you need to examine, including:

- Whether your area is conservative or liberal

- Whether your area leans Republican, Democratic, or neutral

- Which issues your constituents are talking about

- Who the incumbents are and what the voters say about them

Gather most of this information from past election records, which you can obtain through the city and county clerk. Election records will show voter turnout, voter political affiliations, the issues that have been won and lost, and the margins for those elections. This information will provide the most applicable and accurate information because it is based on actions instead of words. Many candidates rely on polls to gather information. However, polls randomly collect information from people, including those who do not vote. Information collected from the clerk's office will provide a clear picture of the people who are voting in your area.

In addition to helping you tailor a campaign, this information will help you decide under which political party you should run. Although this might raise some ethical questions, it is not uncommon for candidates to run under a political party they were not previously affiliated with to increase their potential votes. Obviously, this will not apply to positions that are unaffiliated, or not connected to either political party. For example, the position of coroner is unaffiliated. However, be aware of rules regarding which political party affiliation you can run under. The following table shows which political party you can run under depending on your personal affiliation.

Table 3: Rules on political affiliation and running for office

IF YOU ARE REGISTERED AS A:	AND YOU WANT TO RUN AS A:	ARE YOU ELIGIBLE TO FILE A DECLARATION?
Democrat	Democrat	Yes
Democrat	Republican	No
Democrat	Moderate	No
Democrat	Independent	Yes
Moderate	Moderate	Yes

IF YOU ARE REGISTERED AS A:	AND YOU WANT TO RUN AS A:	ARE YOU ELIGIBLE TO FILE A DECLARATION?
Moderate	Democrat	No
Moderate	Republican	No
Moderate	Independent	Yes
Republican	Republican	Yes
Republican	Democrat	No
Republican	Moderate	No
Republican	Independent	Yes
Independent	Independent	Yes
Independent	Democrat	Yes
Independent	Republican	Yes
Independent	Moderate	Yes

Source: Rhode Island How to Run for Office 2010: A Guide for Candidates, Office of the Secretary of State, A. Ralph Mollis, 2010

If it is imperative for you to run under a political affiliation that you are not allowed to run under, you do have the option to disaffiliate. This means you will officially change your registered party from the one you currently are to the one you wish to run under or to Independent. Disaffiliation must be done at least 90 days before the day you file your declaration of candidacy. This might vary by state, so check your local guidelines to be sure of the requirements in your area.

Conservative versus liberal

If you stopped 100 people on the street and asked them to define a conservative and a liberal, you would probably get 100 different answers. The two terms have been thrown around a lot in the political speak of America. Although they evolve, the terms conservative and liberal do have some concrete attributes associated with them.

Conservatives are on the right side of the political spectrum, which has as its terminus the political theories of monarchy and fascism. Conservatives are not monarchists or fascists, but those are the extremes viewpoints of the political spectrum that conservatives advocate. Communists and socialists are at the extreme end of the liberal political spectrum.

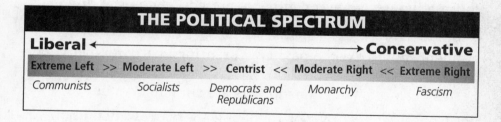

Conservatives believe in small government with limited government interference in daily life in the personal, business, and social spheres. Liberals, on the other hand, believe in a strong government that passes regulations to secure freedoms for all people with government oversight to ensure those freedoms are upheld.

These are the core differences between a Conservative and a Liberal. Over the years, people have tried to attach other criteria to both sides of the argument, including religious leanings, opinions about environmental and defense issues, and cultural values. None of those issues can be applied to defining Conservatives or Liberals. Being Conservative or Liberal involves a political belief of how the government should act, not a definition of how one views social situations.

It is important to view conservative and liberal in their narrow definitions because use of one of the cultural definitions when gauging the political climate of an area can lead to confusion about what your beliefs are. For example, some people associate Conservatives with religion. You might look over your constituency and see many attend church and assume you live in a conservative area. You tailor your message to a platform of small government and less oversight. But you might end up losing because although your constituents are churchgoing individuals, they also advocate a liberal form of government and believe government should exist to pass laws securing liberty for everyone.

In this example, your constituents are churchgoers but they are not Conservatives. By not following the narrow definitions of conservative and liberal, you have misjudged your constituents and sent out a message that is unattractive to them and sabotaged your chances of winning.

Republicans versus Democrats

Political parties are another reason to adopt the narrow definition of Conservatives and Liberals. On the political spectrum, Conservatives and Liberals are situated to the right and left respectively of an area known as centrist. This centrist area consists of political beliefs that do not trend toward either the right or left but borrow from both sides.

Particularly in the United States, most people's political beliefs are centrist. The majority of your constituents are likely to be centrists with beliefs that range from the right to the left with little tendency for radicalization on one side or the other.

It is this centralization of the voting public that makes it necessary for campaigns. If most people were truly a Conservative or Liberal, there would be no need to campaign because the chances of swaying committed ideologues, or staunch advocates of one particular political theory, are low. The side that could get the most voters to turn out would simply win. Most voters do not believe in a certain ideology, such as conservatism or liberalism, but rather vote on issues by using their centrist positioning to listen to the candidate who takes their side on the issue. This is where political parties come in.

In two-party systems, as in the United States, voters can easily weigh candidates against each other. The two political parties will take sides on particular issues facing the electorate, and the voters will vote for the party they agree most with on the issues they feel most strongly about. The political parties themselves also benefit from pursuing a centrist agenda. Some areas of the country historically vote democratic or republican. Because the parties are centrists, candidates in those areas can tailor their message to the voters regardless of party policy, which helps to keep the party in power in that area.

There are several examples of parties using their centrist position to shift their message to secure votes. Bill Clinton used the strategy successfully in 1992 to defeat George H. W. Bush, but John McCain was less successful doing so in 2008 against Barack Obama. In both cases, Clinton and McCain presented voters with a message that was not exactly in line with what their party had put forth in the previous elections. Because the parties are centrist, the candidates could change their message without losing their party designation.

A CLOSER LOOK

John McCain is the most recent and easiest candidate to point to in terms of a politician whose politics occasionally stray from those of his party, yet he continues to win re-election. McCain's chances of being the presidential candidate for the Republican Party in 2008 seemed slim as the primary season started.

McCain hardly had endeared himself to hard-line Republican voters. McCain, the Republican Senator from Arizona, had partnered with Wisconsin Senator and Democrat Russ Feingold to create campaign finance reform, which limited spending and contributions to political campaigns. That did not sit well with many of his Republican counterparts.

But McCain's message did appeal to the larger centrist voting public, and after a surprise win in New Hampshire, which CNN reported was mainly due to Independents voting in the Republican primary, McCain picked up momentum and went on to win the nomination. During the campaign, though, McCain could not keep Independents in his camp. Those votes eventually went to the Democratic nominee, Barack Obama, who won the presidency. Since the election, McCain has not abandoned crossing his party and has made headlines for his stance on health care, the war on terror, and immigration. More recently, McCain has come under fire for these stances.

It is important to know that political parties are centrist because you might live in an area that votes one way or the other. You can still be true to your message and your beliefs regardless of the party you choose. If a political party has a need and is willing to back you, knowing that parties are centrist can help you tailor your message to stay true to your beliefs while still getting the party's support.

Independents

Despite the might of the two main political parties, Independent candidates still have room in the American political system. Of those polled, about 43 percent of Americans consider themselves as independent voters. Most of the smaller offices in local government will be filled by Independents. In a town, village, or small city race, the resources of a major political party will not be needed to win an election. And because the candidate is an Independent, he or she is not considered to be part of any political party.

Running on your own and campaigning in a smaller district will not require party support. For small, local elections, the constituents will likely know you personally or might hear about you through word of mouth. Being attached to a political party might even be a bad idea. In this instance, it is better to run on your reputation and personal connections rather than attaching yourself to a political party.

Suppose a candidate is a well-known shop owner in a town and is running for the village board. The candidate knows many people in the town through his or her personal and business life. The townspeople have already been acquainted with the candidate and would vote for him or her based on their personal experience. The issues facing the town are not ones that need to be defined by political ideology; for example, the village charter sets the size of government, state and federal law determine personal liberties, and the constitution set the rules of government and law.

As you climb up the ladder, however, the role of Independents becomes much more maligned. In larger elections, it is mostly difficult for an Independent to gain a strong following in an area in which the two main political parties have put forth their full force. An Independent cannot compete with the money and traditions of the two major parties, which have been battling it out in one form or another since before the Civil War.

A CLOSER LOOK

Although Independents generally have not made reduced the hold the main political parties have on elections, some Independents have earned public recognition and influenced elections.

Ralph Nader is an example of an Independent who has garnered national attention. Nader has been a candidate for president several times and ran as an Independent in the last two presidential elections. It was as a third-party candidate that Nader got his start. He ran as a third-party candidate from the New Party in the 1970s and more recently as a Green Party candidate in 1996 and 2000. During the 2000 election, when George W. Bush narrowly defeated Al Gore for the presidency, many people blamed Nader's election bid as the reason for Bush's victory. Nader garnered 5 percent of the vote in that election, which only five electoral votes decided.

Recent reviews of the election of 2000 have had mixed conclusions as to whether Nader's candidacy doomed Gore's campaign. Some studies say it had an impact while others conclude those who voted for Nader would not have sided with Gore. Some even suggest his candidacy might have hurt Bush more than Gore in some cases.

In addition, it is important to make a distinction between Independents and third-party candidates. Independent candidates are free from any political party apparatus and are simply running on their own merits and beliefs. One of the most famous examples of an Independent who won an election, which both of the main political parties forcefully contested, was Joe Lieberman in 2008. Lieberman, after losing the Democratic nomination to be Senator of Connecticut, successfully ran as an Independent in the general election against both the Republican contender and the same man who had defeated him in the Democratic primary.

Issues Facing Your Area

In local elections, local issues play the most crucial role in determining the way constituents vote. It is important to be knowledgeable of the issues people in your area are talking about the most. Talking to your possible constituents will be a key way to determine whether you should run and which message you should put forth. As an active member of the community, you should already be aware of some or many of the major issues. However, doing some research can only help you.

Water coolers and coffee clutch

The easiest way to gauge public opinion of issues in your community is simply to listen to conversations going on around you. What are people discussing in the stands at their children's basketball games? What is the conversation at work? What are they saying at the gas station where you grab your cup of coffee in the morning? By simply listening to and asking some questions during these conversations, you can get a pretty good feel for which issues are most important to the people in your area.

Another passive way to collect information is to read the local newspaper consistently and completely. Read the letters to the editor, the police blotter, and everything else your paper has to offer. Read multiple local papers if they cover the area in which you want to run. You should also get involved locally if you are not already. Volunteering on a nonprofit committee or with a nonprofit organization will enable you to passively collect information and make your name more familiar to others. You will be gaining support before you even run.

Attend government meetings

Not all issues that face local government are cause for discussion in public, and some issues your local government might be facing are not well known. By attending government meetings before deciding to run, you can see which issues are facing the government body you want to run for. Attend city council meetings, parks and recreation meetings, and school board meetings. Any meetings that directly affect the community in which you hope to run will give you an advantage.

In addition, you can get campaign ideas while at these meetings. Is there an issue the public needs to know about yet no one is discussing? Raising this issue in your campaign and coming up with a solution is a way to get people talking about you in a positively. It will also let people know you are involved and concerned with the welfare of the community. Knowing you have been involved on a voluntary level will help people trust your intentions rather than view you as just another politician.

CASE STUDY:
ATTENDING GOVERNMENT
MEETINGS INSPIRED ONE
CITIZEN TO RUN FOR OFFICE

Scott Sherwood
City Councilman
Vermilion, Ohio

My interest in politics began in high school when I had the opportunity to attend Buckeye Boy's State my junior year. I served as a deputy clerk in Franklin County municipal court for 10 years before deciding to go back to school and pursue a career in teaching. I have been a teacher and active community member in Vermilion for the past 11 years. I began attending city council meetings about five years ago and became concerned with the direction Vermilion was heading. I ran for council in 2009 and started my first term in 2010.

Although running for city council was a considerable time commitment, I made the decision to do so because I found meetings were counterproductive. I hoped to project a positive businesslike atmosphere and encourage businesses to relocate in Vermilion and build the local economy. While running for council, I made the decision to finance my own campaign. This decision allowed me to spend more time focusing on the issues and less time focusing on fundraising.

Of all the possible campaign techniques, I found yard signs to be the most effective. My opponent in the race was known well in the community, which meant my biggest obstacle was building name recognition. The yard signs demonstrated how much support I had throughout the community, and they got people talking.

The best advice I could give someone interested in pursuing politics is to be aware of the immense time commitment. My job is 24 hours per day, and it is not out of the realm of possibility to get phone calls day or night. Part of my success as a candidate can be attributed to having a supportive partner. My wife has been supportive of my efforts, and it makes a difference. Political campaigns and serving as a politician can be stressful. Having a supportive partner makes the entire process easier to endure.

The Role of Incumbency

One rule of politics is that incumbents are hard to beat. Since the mid-70s, with few exceptions, over 90 percent of all Congressional incumbents running for re-election have won their campaign. This shows how daunting a task it is to unseat a popular incumbent.

So what makes incumbents so unbeatable? The first aspect is name recognition. Most incumbents are known by their constituents, who are more likely to vote for a name they know rather than one they do not on a ballot no matter what the credentials of each happen to be.

Secondly, most voters, unless the incumbent has voted for something unpopular, believe their own representative is doing a good job. Also, especially in local elections, incumbents simply run unchallenged. An unpopular town supervisor or city council member might keep his or her seat because no one chooses to run against him or her.

When facing an incumbent, you must first determine whether that incumbent is popular or whether people are looking for a change. If the voters are happy with the incumbent's performance, it will be difficult to beat that incumbent. This does not mean you should not try; it is simply a cautionary warning.

If they are not happy, the next step is to get your name out there as the alternative to the unpopular incumbent. By showing how different you are from the incumbent, you can garner votes and mobilize supporters and voters who would normally not show up at the polls. The most crucial step you must take is getting your name into the minds of voters. Voters will not vote for someone they do not know.

Making the Decision to Run

At this point, you have had the opportunity to decide whether you want to — and should — run for a political office. The following checklist will help you to make your final decision. Once you have decided to run, you still have a lot of work to do before submitting your declaration of candidacy if you hope to run a successful campaign.

☑ CHAPTER CHECKLIST

☐ Answer the questions posed in the first part of this chapter.

☐ Write down your political goals.

☐ Chose the elected position you want to run for.

☐ Collect information from the clerk's office about the voter activity in past elections for this position.

☐ Decide which political affiliation you want to run under, if any.

☐ Disaffiliate from your current political party if you need to.

☐ Attend government meetings and passively collect information about issues within the community.

☐ Make a list of the issues and goals in your community.

☐ Compare the list of community issues with your political goals.

☐ Look into who is currently holding the position.

☐ Find out whether that person is eligible for re-election.

☐ Find out how many times the incumbent has been elected to that position.

☐ Find out whether the incumbent is popular with citizens. All this information will be necessary as you assemble your campaign plan. *The campaign plan will be explained fully in Chapter 4.*

CHAPTER 3

Assembling Your Team

Your team is going to be the small group of professionals who will work with you from the day you declare your candidacy until the day you are elected. These people will handle your schedule, finances, fundraisers, image, and volunteers among other things. You will depend on them to adhere to your campaign strategy and work in your best interest. Assembling a core team you can trust is essential to winning an election. Even a small election can be time consuming and mentally and emotionally draining on a candidate.

At least your team should include a professional campaign manager, public relations specialist, and treasurer. The larger the election and campaign, the greater need you will have for additional help. For example, you might also need a fundraising coordinator, volunteer coordinator, communications director, political director, campaign committee, and volunteers. It is highly recommended you do not enlist family members to fill these positions. Family members create a conflict of interest. They will bring strong emotions into the campaign and are not always capable of making decisions that are truly best for the campaign. The family is an important aspect of the team on its own.

Campaign Manager

The campaign manager does exactly as their name suggests: They manage the campaign. The campaign manager is the go-to person for every candidate. The campaign manager should be the first team member assembled because he or she will be the most important. Find a campaign manager before officially entering the election because the manager will help create the campaign strategy, which should be in place when you first begin to campaign. The campaign strategy is going to be the step-by-step guide for the entire campaign and will include the campaign's and candidate's goals, strengths, weaknesses, donors, fundraising efforts, and more. *Your campaign strategy will be discussed further in Chapter 4.*

Day-to-day operations

The campaign manager runs all the daily operations of your campaign. Think of the campaign manager as the CEO of your campaign. You are still president of the company, but your campaign manager is running everything. As you add more members to your team, the campaign manager will act as a buffer between you and everyone else. This will prevent you from being bombarded with questions and problems you do not have time or the power to deal with.

Campaign managers must be organized individuals to keep everything running smoothly. For bigger elections, these individuals might oversee a large staff sometimes numbering in the hundreds. For smaller elections, a campaign manager takes on more roles him or herself and focuses on the tasks, including coordinating volunteers, coordinating fundraising efforts, and managing your schedule, that need to be done to keep your campaign running smoothly, .

Focus on running for office

Time must be spent on expense reports, disclosures, and other items law requires from a candidate. All this paperwork can impinge on the time a candidate needs to focus on the campaign itself. This is where a campaign manager can be helpful. A campaign manager can handle much of this paperwork and free up the candidate to focus on his or her platform and the message he or she wants to send to the public. The campaign manager will also make sure all required paperwork is filed correctly and on time. This will eliminate the risk of being disqualified for not adhering to election laws. A candidate who does not need to worry about filing expense reports or disclosing new campaign funds can better focus on the issues that are important to his or her image.

Connections to the political system

Campaign managers often have a background in the local political system, which means they might have connections to some local political figures. This can help your campaign in many ways. In addition to giving you a pipeline for seeking endorsements, learning the real issues facing local government, and meeting with the bureaucracy, these connections can give you a resource for election advice. These current political figures have successfully won elections in the area in which you are trying to get elected. Taking the time to ask them questions about what worked for them, how to best mobilize your support, and which issues are considered hot-button issues will increase your knowledge going into a campaign. This also will give your campaign credibility in the eyes of the voters because you are associating with people they trust and have voted for in the past.

 A CLOSER LOOK

The use of campaign managers can make a big difference in campaigns, especially if you are not able to foresee some of the issues your campaign will face.

When Richard Blumenthal of Connecticut put his name into the ring to run in the 2010 mid-term election for a Senate seat Christopher Dodd vacated, a *New York Times* article suggested he would "glide" into the seat.

Blumenthal is a popular attorney general in the state and a consumer advocate who, for the last 20 years, has worked for the people of Connecticut. Because of this, Blumenthal was an attractive choice for Democrats.

However, Blumenthal's campaign was defined by a series of missteps and blunders.

According to the sources the *Times* talked with, Blumenthal was unprepared to handle going head-to-head with other candidates.

"Mr. Blumenthal flopped in his first televised debate against an obscure primary opponent, and he is ruling out any possibility of a rematch," the article said.

What attributed to this seasoned politician's failure in a debate? The *Times* talked with a senior Democratic official who said the reason could be Blumenthal's job as attorney general.

"[Peter] Kelly said years of one-sided news conferences had left the attorney general unaccustomed to challenge. 'He's got to be able to take attacks, deal with them appropriately, and hand them back,' Mr. Kelly said. 'He's not really been tested at that.'"

His most likely opponent in the election had good name recognition, which also had Blumenthal and Democrats worried.

Linda McMahon got the Republican nomination. As the wife of Vince McMahon and a mogul in the wrestling entertainment industry, she had more instant name recognition due to her entertainment connections than Blumenthal with his political popularity.

To combat these questions and doubts, Blumenthal turned to an experienced campaign manager to help turn things around, according to the *Times*.

Blumenthal hired Mindy Myers, who has experience on several levels. She ran President Barack Obama's campaign in New Hampshire and serves as chief of staff for Senator Sheldon Whitehouse of Rhode Island.

She was also described in Suzanne Charlé's Blog as "a veteran of tough, tight campaigns." She also spent time working on Al Gore's presidential campaign and working in the Bill Clinton White House and for Senator Tom Daschle.

And it seems as though hiring Myers paid off. Blumenthal successfully won the election.

Public Relations Specialists

The most important thing in a local election is name recognition. When voters go to the polls, if they do not recognize your name on the ballot, chances are they will not vote for you. The job of a public relations specialist is to disperse information about you and your platform to the public.

Public relations experts are highly specialized in their fields. They do not run campaigns, they do not manage the money flow of your campaign, and they do not advise on policy. What they do know, however, is how to work with media outlets to get your name, face, and message out in front of the people. Public relations specialists can also advise candidates about their physical appearance and clothing choices. They oversee the candidate photos used for campaign literature and advertisements and control how the public receives your image.

Many public relations specialists will work for you on a part-time or as-needed basis. Many work as independent consultants and are not part of a big business. This can be beneficial for small campaigns for which hiring a full-time public relations expert does not make sense but getting help relaying well-crafted messages can go a long way.

Professional messages

Appearance is everything when it comes to campaigning. As a candidate, you should talk with people and listen to them while sticking to your main message and platform. You should also be prepared, confident, and unrattled by any circumstance.

Public relations specialists can help create this appearance. By working with a public relations specialist, you can have your message crafted in a professional way that most people will receive well. The public relations expert can create newspaper ads, speeches, scripts for radio or television spots, and a wide range of other promotional materials, such as brochures and yard signs.

Public relations specialists deal with more than words and scripts. They can give advice on appearance and the best ways to campaign in certain areas and tips on how you should interact with people. Finding a public relations specialist with political experience is a plus, but if he or she charges more than you are willing to spend, any public relations specialist should have the knowledge and skill to do the job.

Avoid costly slip-ups

Public relations specialists can help you avoid slip-ups that could cost you an election. Blundering speeches, not adhering to a cohesive message, or not realizing the political leanings of a group you are addressing could all prove to be fatal for a campaign.

Small details, such as your appearance, can make a big difference in an election, and public relations specialists can help you determine the look you need.

Experience with the media

In addition, public relations specialists have a good working relationship with the local news media, which can improve your contacts with this outlet. Being helpful and accessible to the media can be a big boost for your campaign, and public relations specialists can help you take that to the next level.

One aspect of their job is to make sure every positive thing you do is communicated to the news media. It might be something small that you would never think to tell the media about, but a public relations expert will recognize it as an opportunity.

For example, suppose you are an active runner who has run for several charity events. A public relations specialist can help you play up this hobby in several ways. First of all, you are physically fit, which means you have something many people want out of their elected officials: discipline. You will not stray from the task at hand; you will not be distracted. Secondly, you give your time to help those in need. The public will vote for someone with strong morals who puts others in front of themselves. A good public relations specialist will make sure the public notices these aspects during your campaign.

In addition, public relations specialists can give to news organizations ideas for stories for which you would be a good source.

News reporters are always looking for ideas and might appreciate when someone presents them with an idea they simply have to follow up on.

Treasurer

Having a campaign treasurer is essential to all elections regardless of the size. Most states require each campaign to have a treasurer who is not the candidate fill out forms, collect money, and stay updated on the required forms. Someone in this position should have good math and managerial skills and be trustworthy in both your eyes and the eyes of the public. Every financial move is carefully recorded during elections. An innocent mistake in paperwork can be spun to look as though a candidate was hiding money and donations or stealing. For a candidate overwhelmed with the process of running a successful campaign, mistakes in paperwork happen easily. Hiring a treasurer with professional experience will ensure mistakes are unlikely and the money is being carefully recorded. A treasurer will also help the candidate set a budget, adhere to that budget, and determine the success of his or her fundraising efforts.

Fundraising Coordinator

The fundraising coordinator will oversee all fundraising activities, which include soliciting donors, collecting money, and planning events. A successful fundraising coordinator will be aware of the type of events that raise the most money, and he or she will have a track record of planning such events. Fundraising activities should be varied in size and complexity to appeal to a wider audience. The fundraising coordinator will plan these efforts at all levels. *Types of fundraising events and their potential success will be discussed further in Chapter 5.* The fundraising coordinator needs to be detail oriented, outgoing, and a solid communicator.

Volunteer Coordinator

The volunteer coordinator is an important position because volunteers are essential to the success of any campaign. The volunteer coordinator will recruit volunteers, assess how each volunteer can best help the campaign, contact volunteers when needed, organize volunteers at events and rallies, and provide motivation and encouragement to the volunteers. An important role of the volunteer coordinator is making each volunteer feel his or her personal contributions are essential to the campaign. It is also the volunteer coordinator's job to act as a liaison between the volunteers and the candidate.

Communications Director

The communications director will be the liaison between the candidate and the media through all written material and statements released on your behalf. This person prepares press releases and speeches for the candidate that are intended to be used on the Internet and in television, newspaper, and radio. A communications director might not be needed in smaller elections for which the media does not play a prominent role. Additionally, in smaller elections, the role of the communications director can be combined with the public relations specialist. However, when a public relations specialist is also a member of the team, the communications director will focus on written communication while the public relations specialist focuses on everything else having to do with your image and how your message is delivered.

DEVELOPING A COMMUNICATIONS PLAN

To prepare for the media involvement related to an election, it is important to develop a communications plan. The following steps will walk you through the creation of a solid communications plan.

1. Background information: Compile all information about the candidate and campaign that can be used during media communications. This information will be compiled during the research for the campaign strategy and should be readily available.

2. Campaign message: Include a typed copy of the official campaign message in the communications plan along with a few key related points.

3. Goals: Include a written list of goals the candidate is planning to achieve if elected.

4. Audience: Compile a list of all local media outlets and their contact information. Having this information ready will quicken the process when press releases are being distributed.

5. List of tactics: This lists the primary methods by which the candidate plans to distribute their message.

6. Evaluation: After each media encounter, the candidate and communications director should determine whether the experience was particularly positive or negative. The campaign strategy can be adjusted to accommodate either experience.

Political Director

Political directors are found in elections at the county level and beyond. In a large campaign, the political director takes on the responsibility of overseeing the team. In smaller elections, the campaign manager oversees the team and acts as a liaison between the team and the candidate. In larger elections, this responsibility falls to the political director so the campaign manager can focus more of his or her time and energy on the candidate and make sure everything is going according to the campaign strategy they created.

Scheduler

The scheduler also has an important job, which is keeping the candidate's schedule and letting the candidate know where he or she needs to be and when. During a campaign, the schedule of events and appearances will often change with little notice. The scheduler will be in charge of keeping the schedule updated, scheduling appearances with groups requesting your presence, and letting you know the name of the group you are about to speak in front of. The scheduler keeps track of everything from fundraisers and debates to doctor's appointments if they should fall during the election. The scheduler communicates directly with the candidate. He or she lets the candidate know how long to stay at each event, and the scheduler is able to account for travel time in the schedule. It is common for a candidate to have multiple meetings, events, and functions that he or she will be expected to attend in a single day. It is the scheduler's job to make sure that happens. Once again, the larger a campaign is, the more essential the role of a scheduler becomes.

Family

Although family should not have specific jobs within the campaign, the family plays an essential role in the campaign. It is the family's job to be present and be supportive. The family should attend political rallies and important fundraisers. The family also represents the candidate's personal life, which might include being pictured in election advertisements. During elections, it is important that family members act in such a way that appropriately represents the candidate.

Campaign Community

The campaign community includes members of the community who are influential and agree to publicly support the candidate. Although they do not work directly for the campaign, they are donors and help promote the candidate at fundraising events and community functions. This can include sponsoring their own fundraisers on behalf of the candidate. It is important for the candidate to work closely with the campaign community. Offending members of this group can result in their loyalties switching to the opponent.

Volunteers

Running for political office is more than just putting up signs and handing out leaflets at local events. To get your name out to the public, you need to develop a network of people who will help spread your message, give you advice, and donate their time to help you obtain the office you seek. When recruiting volunteers, let people know that any time or resources they can offer will be appreciated. If people feel as though they will be tasked with too much, they might not be willing to help.

Also, you should sell them on the idea of your candidacy. Show them what you can do for the town as a whole and for them personally. Let them know their hard work will be rewarded by an elected official who has their needs in mind. Always be gracious for whatever support you receive. You might ask someone to volunteer and receive a donation or an endorsement instead. By being thankful and gracious, you will get another vote in your corner, and they might even help you by spreading your candidacy through word of mouth.

Volunteers and community involvement

Volunteers are the lifeblood of any campaign. Volunteers are people you meet who believe strongly in the message you are putting forth. They believe in where you stand on issues. The people in your life who encourage you to run or help you make the decision to run are the people who will likely be the first to volunteer for your campaign. Remember those discussions at the morning coffee shop or the basketball game? They are opportunities to test the support you would receive if you ran for office.

Letting people know you are thinking about running for office and watching their reaction can be a way to gauge your support. Make a statement such as, "I have been listening to what you have been saying, and I think I would like to run for office and make those changes." Not only are you embracing their message, but you have already proved you are listening to them and have their concerns at the forefront of your mind. If the group seems excited to see you run, there is a good chance the community as a whole would support your platform.

Volunteers are an essential part of all campaigns, regardless of how large or small the campaign is. Volunteers are the people who conduct polls, make phone calls, keep up with office work, distribute information and signs, and collect signatures on the nomination petitions. There is no way a candidate would have the time or energy to do all the necessary work required in a campaign without the help of volunteers. Additionally, volunteers come with a wide variety of skills and talents. It is important that the volunteer coordinator best use each volunteer. It is also important for the candidate to maintain contact with the volunteers as a group to ensure they feel appreciated and part of something bigger.

Recruiting volunteers

Anyone who feels the least bit inclined to volunteer should be accepted. You do not want to alienate potential voters by not allowing them to volunteer for your campaign. Volunteers will be some of your greatest influences with other voters because they will be the ones talking about you in a positive light to others. Ask your volunteers to invite their family and friends to different events or to volunteer as well. Make sure every volunteer gives you all their contact information.

In addition to family and friends, consider approaching groups that are likely to vote for you based on your stance on specific issues. Some groups are more likely than others to vote for a candidate based on one or two issues. These groups include veterans, environmentalist, pro-abortion or anti-abortion groups, seniors, land-use advocates, union workers, gay rights groups or anti-gay rights groups, firearm advocates, and hunters. Find the groups that are likely to support your stance on the issues directly affecting them.

Keeping volunteers happy

There are things a candidate should and should not do to best use their volunteers and keep their volunteers happy and feeling like vital parts of the campaign. Taking volunteers for granted, not supplying them with adequate information, or not providing them appropriate training are all ways to alienate and eventually lose volunteers. Losing volunteers will also lead to a loss in votes. Your volunteers are also voters.

First, volunteer meetings and events should always start on time. Consistently starting things late will encourage volunteers to show up late and make the volunteers who showed up on time feel as though they are wasting their time. Starting and ending meetings on time will show the volunteers you value their time and feel their time is just as important as yours.

Secondly, the volunteers should be clearly informed of the task that needs to be accomplished. This will allow the volunteers to be mentally prepared but also to bow out if it is an activity they are not comfortable doing. For example, not all volunteers will be comfortable canvassing door to door. It is important to never make a volunteer feel pressured to do a job he or she is not comfortable doing. This will lead to not performing the job well and possibly becoming resentful.

It is also important to let volunteers know well in advance if they need to bring anything with them to an activity or event, and if they will be outside, you should let them know in advance so they can dress for the weather. People do not like feeling unprepared for things, and volunteers in a political campaign are no exception. Creating a situation in which volunteers show up unprepared will delay the task and possibly lead to a loss of repeat volunteers.

Volunteer activities should also be well organized. For example, if you are asking people to take time out of their day to prepare a mailing, you should have all the supplies and addresses they will need ready and organized. This will save time and energy. The job will get done faster, and the volunteers will leave feeling as though they accomplished something.

Volunteers also need to be matched to appropriate jobs. It would be highly ineffective to assign a shy individual to a phone bank just as it would be ineffective to have an outgoing person stuck in an office stuffing envelopes. Talk to the volunteers ahead of time to see how they would like to spend their time. Assessing a volunteer's skills and abilities is as simple as a brief interview or even a questionnaire.

Keep volunteers informed of events or changes throughout the campaign. Make sure volunteers know where to go if they have a question or need help with the task they have been assigned. If times or locations have changed, it is important to contact every volunteer rather than leave a message and hope the information gets to everyone.

Treat the volunteers as though they are paid employees. In many situations, volunteers are not appreciated for the immense amount of work they do. In larger elections, the volunteers often do not even get to meet the actual candidate. Do your best to meet volunteers and thank them for their hard work. If that is not possible, hire a volunteer coordinator who is prepared to actively work with and talk to volunteers. Your volunteer coordinator will represent you to the volunteers.

Do not reprimand volunteers for not showing up to an event or criticize them for not doing a job perfectly. Sometimes people volunteer because they have good intentions, but they are just too busy to be involved. Drawing attention to the fact they did not follow through on a commitment will likely lead to them feeling offended. If you are unhappy with a volunteer's work or lack of effort, simply take their name off the volunteer list.

When volunteers are working for long periods of time or over a meal period, have food available. This can be as simple as ordering a meat and cheese tray from a local grocery store or asking another volunteer to make a pot of sloppy joes to bring to the activity. You do not want volunteers leaving grumpy and hungry.

Avoid letting volunteers take work home. You do not want literature you paid to have printed getting lost or ruined. Although volunteers would not intentionally ruin something, accidents happen, especially if the volunteer has young children or pets at home. Schedule times for volunteer work at the campaign headquarters or other designated location.

Keep a record of volunteers who showed up for different events and activities so you can thank the appropriate people. After the campaign is over, regardless of whether you won or lost, you should send thank-you cards to your volunteers. Thanking volunteers for specific activities they participated in or goals they accomplished will make them feel their work was noticed.

The following is a list of potential tasks a volunteer can complete:

- Designing graphics and printed materials
- Conducting background research
- Canvassing door to door
- Addressing envelopes
- Making copies
- Distributing fliers at public events
- Distributing yard signs
- Assisting at fundraising events
- Soliciting campaign contributions
- Stuffing envelopes
- Making signs
- Writing press releases
- Monitoring the newspapers and local news
- Recruiting other volunteers
- Making phone calls
- Conducting surveys
- Manning booths at public events
- Watching the polls
- Driving voters to the polls
- Running errands
- Preparing food for events
- Helping plan public events
- Setting up and tearing down for events
- Organizing meetings
- Keeping records
- Fulfilling needed positions on the candidate's team

Training volunteers

Volunteer jobs should be divided into small manageable activities. For example, if you need envelopes stuffed and addressed, have one set of volunteers addressing the envelopes and a separate set of volunteers stuffing the envelopes. Also, if the list of addresses you want to send mail to is several pages long, divide the list into manageable numbers. Giving volunteers too much work will discourage them. When the tasks are broken into small manageable tasks, the training should be fairly simple.

However, there are other tasks, such as phone calls and door-to-door canvassing, which will require more training. For example, volunteers will need to know what to do if no one answers, where they are allowed to leave campaign literature, and what to do when an angry individual confronts them. Volunteers need to remain calm and diplomatic at all times. Providing the volunteers with information on how to respond to various questions and situations will enable them to feel confident and prepared when representing the candidate. It is also important to regularly remind volunteers they are representing the candidate, so the way they dress, act, and speak while volunteering is important.

Rewarding volunteers

Volunteers should be rewarded with frequent praise and gratitude. Volunteers who have stepped into leadership roles should be fully recognized for their effort and possibly given a title to reflect their level of responsibility. Following the campaign, volunteers should be invited to the win or loss party, and they should

be sent thank-you cards. Even if you lose the election, it is important to keep a positive relationship with your volunteers. They
might be vital to you in future campaigns.

Downfalls of Hiring Professionals

There are downfalls to relying on professionals to accomplish
something as important and personal as winning an election.
However, using professional help is essential to a successful campaign. The secret to avoiding these downfalls is to hire people
you can trust who have plenty of related experience. Avoid the
temptation to cut corners or let family members and friends take
on jobs because you feel obligated to include them.

Not always in control of the message

For the most part, election professionals should keep their opinions about the issues to themselves unless you directly ask for
their views. A campaign manager might be more politically bi-
ased if he or she works for one political party over the other. Nev-
ertheless, you should aim to hire professionals who are apolitical
and will work on the details of your campaign instead of spread
political ideology.

When working with a professional, know that your name is still
on the product. If your campaign manager, treasurer, or public
relations guru makes a public mistake, it is going to come down

on you, which relates to the top pitfall of hiring a professional: You are not always in control of the message. Your staff is out there in the public eye as well, and anything they say or do will reflect on you and your campaign. A good candidate will carefully read, edit, and approve any item that is being sent out to the public.

Relying on others to do what is in your best interest

You have hired these professionals, and you pay them to act in your best interest, but this does not mean they will always do so. The professionals you hire are consultants. They can give you their advice based on their experience and knowledge of the system, but it is up to you to make the decisions. You are in charge of your campaign and will take the heat if anything goes wrong. No matter how good the intentions, the advice of these professionals can be wrong.

Cost

There is no getting around the fact that money plays a huge role in a campaign at any level, from town hall to county to Congress. Hiring professionals is a necessary expense. Include this cost in your proposed budget to get a realistic picture of how much money you will need to run a successful campaign. Also, consider your volunteers as potential resources. If money is truly a problem and you cannot afford to hire a professional to fill every position, consider your pool of volunteers. You might have an event coordinator among your volunteers who can oversee planning and organizing your fundraising events. Likewise, you might have a freelance writer among your volunteers who is willing to write your press releases. Carefully consider all your options.

CASE STUDY:
PROFESSIONAL CAMPAIGN
MANAGER OFFERS ADVICE
TO POTENTIAL CANDIDATES

The Campaign Manager
http://campaignmanager.blogspot.com

Are campaign managers necessary?

There is an old saying: The lawyer who represents himself has a fool for a client. It is the same way with campaigns. I am a smart guy; I know what I'm doing. But if I ran for office, I would still find someone to be my campaign manager. It is too important to have a day-to-day figure who is both inside the entire process but also, in another sense, outside.

When a candidate gets mad at me, one of the things I often hear is, "It's not your name on the ballot." That is true, but this is also what gives a manager, be he ever so inexperienced, that ability to see things differently. Candidates naturally believe they are right. They naturally believe they ought to get the support of the overwhelming majority of the electorate.

In the first case, let me just say that being right has never been enough on its own to get you across the finish line. In the second case, if this is a truly competitive race, you will not be getting 80 to 90 percent of the vote. A certain number of voters are simply not going to support you.

A manager is the person who makes sure, in a small race, you do not go to that door or, in a larger race, do not target that demographic in television ads. A manager is just sufficiently outside to have some perspective a candidate will not have. A manager also helps candidates manage their time so they do not try to be everywhere and all things to all people — something candidates are prone to try.

I will offer one caveat: I say it is important to have a manager, but I do not agree it is always important to hire a professional campaign manager. If you are running in a small race, for example a city council race that will cost $10,000 to run, spending money on professional staff is just senseless. Save that money for direct voter contact. In those cases, a campaign manager can be a friend or relative — someone trusted and intelligent who will work for free or a pittance.

Tasks a campaign manager handles

The basic staff structure, in order of importance, is as follows:

- Campaign manager
- Finance director
- Field director
- Communications director
- New media director
- Research director

In a large campaign, you might have deputies and assistants for each of these positions. Often, if you have a deputy campaign manager, they will take ownership of a particular aspect of the campaign. But as a general rule, the campaign manager is responsible for seeing all these areas are handled. In a smaller race, in which the only full-time staff member is often the campaign manager, he or she must perform some part of all these aspects of a campaign.

If you want to state it simply, the campaign manager is responsible for managing the candidate's resources, especially the candidate's time. I emphasize time because time is the single nonrenewable resource. You can raise more money, recruit more volunteers, and run more ads, but you can never increase the number of hours between now and when the polls close. A manager must keep the candidate focused on making the most efficient use of his or her resources and taking into account the limited time available. This means not wasting time on voters who will never support the candidate, not wasting time on donors who are not going to write any more checks, and not straying from the determined message.

Hiring other professionals

Almost every campaign needs a treasurer. As a rule, this is not a paid position. It is filled by a close volunteer and friend of the candidate who is often also a lawyer or accountant. This person holds a statutory role rather a professional campaign-management role.

Depending on the size of the race, the next professional to be hired after a manager is either a fundraiser or a field organizer. It is not uncommon for a midsize legislative race to, for example, cede some of the responsibilities for fundraising to a financial consultant. In that case, it will be the consultant's main job to craft solicitations and build lists, which will include contact and some general information and the amount they can be expected to contribute, but it is still the job of the campaign — and the candidate and manager — to ask.

The reason a candidate might not hire a full-time finance director in this case is because he or she can hire a field director who has little or no experience, give them on-the-job training, and still expect them to do a decent job. Frankly, if you hire a finance director who has not done it before, you are in for a rude shock.

The basis of a campaign is direct voter contact, which includes paid media, such as targeted television and radio ads, direct mail, and online advertising, but does not include yard signs or T-shirts. For this, you do need at least a professional graphic designer and a printer. For bigger television buys, you will also want a media buyer, who is often also the same person who creates the ad.

Effective campaign strategies

I believe in the K.I.S.S. rule — Keep It Simple, Stupid — especially in smaller races. You need to find the people who are going to vote for you and then make sure they vote. That is all there is to it. You win by direct voter contact, including knocking on doors, making phone calls, sending direct mail pieces, and running ads. It does not include yard signs, bumper stickers, or T-shirts, so do not get caught up in trying to be fancy.

When I hear someone tell me they want to try something different, I get nervous. Before Jackson Pollock did his splatter and drip painting, which I love, he learned how to draw and paint in a traditional style. That is the reasons it looks terrible when I try and replicate his famous canvasses. I never learned how to paint first.

And when I hear "outside of the box," it is often from someone who never bothered to learn what was in the box first. You can be creative, but you should take care of the basics first. Smart people created the box. They might not have all the answers, but listen to what they have to say and learn from them before you dismiss it.

Mudslinging

The term mudslinging is tossed about too much. Like most folks in politics, I refer to it as either negative advertising or comparative advertising. Done properly, it is absolutely ethical and moral. Done inappropriately, it becomes ugly and unprofessional.

Consider this example: You support policy A. Your opponent opposes policy A. You think you are right and he is wrong and the voters will agree, so you say, via earned and paid media, "My opponent opposes A and that opposition is a bad thing." Voila, that is negative campaigning.

If you are in possession of some negative information about your opponent, it is not always a bad thing to release it. The voters do have a right to know about the candidates, including the reason your opponent might not be right for the job. Is your opponent behind on their property taxes? That says something about him. Does he vote in every election? The answer to that surely reflects on his true level of civic engagement. Does he have a criminal record? If he is already a legislator, has he voted to cut services for seniors or funding for local schools? Has he been lying about something?

Use your judgment in deciding where to draw the line. If he is divorced and started dating his current girlfriend before the divorce was finalized, you should probably consider that it does not significantly reflect on his character. If, like David Vitter, he was using prostitutes while running as a family values candidate, then by all means, put it out there.

Take my advice

Especially at the local level, just do it. It is a good experience. It's also a learning experience. You might fall down the first time, but you will be better at it if you choose to try again.

Yes, you should talk with family and friends about what it will mean, but do not blow things out of proportion. If you win your local city council race, *Meet the Press* will not be inviting you to speak, most folks still will not recognize you, and the local newspaper will not be calling you that much. Winning will make you a city council member, not a target of the paparazzi.

Moving Forward with your Team

Once you have your team of professionals assembled, you will be able to get to work on your campaign. Your campaign strategy will need to be created first. However, from there, your various team members will have their own goals and objectives to accomplish simultaneously. The next step in the process is declaring your candidacy. The following checklist will walk you through building your team quickly and effectively.

☑ CHAPTER CHECKLIST

☐ Hire a campaign manager.

☐ With the campaign manager, decide which other professionals will be needed based on the size of your campaign.

☐ Hire the remaining needed professionals.

☐ Have a meeting with everyone to create team cohesion and make sure everyone understands you and your message.

☐ Create volunteer recruiting cards.

☐ Begin recruiting volunteers for the campaign.

CHAPTER 4

Throwing Your Hat into the Ring

There is a fair amount of paperwork involved in deciding to run in an election. The various forms will be outlined in this chapter. You can obtain all the forms you will need by contacting the city or your county clerk. It is vitally important to know and understand the election laws in your area and applicable state and federal election laws. After filling out the appropriate paperwork, you will need to declare your candidacy to the public and officially start your campaign. This is an exciting step in the election process, and a good kickoff event can put a campaign on the fast track to success.

Knowing Election Laws

Election laws vary from state to state and municipality to municipality, and they can be complicated. Knowing the laws of your individual area is important to running a successful campaign.

Many municipalities will hold candidate workshops once the nomination period is over to discuss campaign laws and other issues specific to that municipality. Ask your local clerk about the times of the workshops and attend them to avoid running a campaign that conflicts with these laws.

In addition, public libraries have records of all the laws regarding elections in your area. If you have any questions about whether what you are doing is legal, you should consult these legal references. The Internet can be another source of information, but election laws change from state to state so do not rely on advice if the information is not state-specific.

Breaking election laws is a serious offense, and little leniency is given to those who break them. Always err on the side of caution, especially when it comes to disclosing financial contributions and support. Nothing will derail a campaign quicker than a candidate who has an air of financial impropriety about them.

Work with your local clerk if you have any questions because he or she can advise you. The clerk is an expert on election laws and is the head of the office that oversees elections. However, do not assume the clerk is in your favor. If you do not ask the right questions, you might not get all the information you need. Get copies of all the information you need, including election laws, in writing. This will protect you from supporters of your opponent who want to lead you astray.

CASE STUDY:
A LOOK AT WHAT
IS NEEDED TO RUN
A SUCCESSFUL CAMPAIGN

Barry Lepler
blepler2994@wowway.com

A political campaign needs four things to be successful. The first is money. Senator Mark Hanna, the Karl Rove and David Axelrod of his day, was once asked, "Senator, what is the secret of political success?" He replied, "There are two. The first is money, and I forgot the second." A candidate needs enough money and must be the one with the most to win. The second factor is time. A candidate must lead by example and make his or her campaign the dominant part of his or her life for a period. How can a candidate ask others to help if he or she does not work hard? The third factor is having a plan. The calendar dictates what you should do and when. You cannot control what other candidates do; you can only control yourself. The fourth factor is involving others. Volunteers, and possibly paid staff, expand the candidate's effort. Giving people responsibility for different parts of the campaign will attract others to help. Each factor has tasks to fulfill, but there is a difference between the desire to hold a position and the ability to be a good person and produce a campaign that wins.

How to File to be a Candidate

Municipalities have certain nomination periods during which candidates must declare they intend to run for office to have their names put on the ballots. You can watch the newspaper or your local government websites to find out when these times are, or you can contact your local clerk of courts for this information. Nomination periods are often a couple of months before the primary election. If your area's primary election is in April, the nomination deadline could be in February. However, some municipalities have different deadlines. Call your city or county clerk to get a list of important dates for the election process in your area.

Nomination papers are a series of forms you must fill out so the town, village, city, or county clerk can check your records to make sure you are an eligible candidate for the position you want to run for. The clerk will check what district you live in, whether you are a resident of the area and the length of time you have lived there, and your criminal history.

Nominating petition

Some elected positions require nominating petitions. Citizens sign this petition that says they would like to see you run for the position. This does not mean they will vote for you, it just says they believe you are capable and you would make a good candidate. Find out from your area's clerk of courts how many valid signatures you will need and what is required for the signature to be considered valid. Requirements for a valid signature will likely include the individual's full legal name and mailing address. Each individual will need to be over 18, a registered voter, and a resident of the voting district of the candidate.

Know the rules and regulations for the petitions. Every signature will be checked to ensure it is legitimate, and it will be verified that you have the correct minimum number. Once you know what is required, properly train the volunteers who will be collecting signatures to make sure they get all the needed information written correctly on the form. Collect more signatures than needed just in case some are declared invalid. For example, if you need 400 signatures, collect 450. Collecting more than the minimum needed amount carries no penalties. Also, turn your petition forms in as early as possible. This will allow you to fix any mistakes or collect additional signatures if needed.

You can begin campaigning while seeking petitions because you and your volunteers will have a chance to talk to prospective voters during this time.

Monetary disclosure forms

Disclosure forms are required in nearly every election, and most deal with financial issues. Candidates are asked to disclose the amount of campaign funds they have received, the way they will fund their campaigns, and their contributors' identity. As the campaign continues, the clerk's office will direct you to file more of these forms. These disclosure forms also include any economic ties the candidate has to the city and any government officials or committees who are backing the candidate. Candidates will also be required to disclose sources of income and personal assets and assets of their spouse and dependent children. Finally, the candidate will be required to disclose any person, business, or organization owed more than $1,000 by the candidate, his or her spouse, or his or her dependent children.

Along with the disclosure form, some municipalities ask for a statement of qualifications that will be included in your candidacy file. This statement will include your reasons for running for office, the skills you offer, and your relevant experiences. Honesty is important when filling out these forms because they will be public record throughout your candidacy and the media and the public can check them. The clerk's office will make all these documents available to the public for inspection both while you are running and during office.

Announcing Your Candidacy

Another important aspect of running for political office is announcing your candidacy to the public. This could be at a dinner with a group of supporters, or it could be through a public media outlet. The bigger the office, the bigger the announcement. When Arnold Schwarzenegger announced his candidacy for the governor of California, he did so on Jay Leno's television show. This created an instant buzz around his campaign. Although running for a city council member position in a small town might not warrant a guest spot on "The Tonight Show," it might warrant an opening rally to begin building excitement.

PRESS RELEASES

A press release is a specially formatted statement sent to news sources to inform the editors or reporters of a newsworthy event or person. Press releases are written in third person and provide brief, yet complete, information about the person or event. Many candidates announce their candidacy by sending a press release to the local papers and television news stations. Press releases can also be used to announce upcoming rallies and fundraising events. Those news sources will then contact the candidate for more information or an interview. It is acceptable to send press releases by fax, e-mail, or traditional mail.

There are certain components that are expected to be in every press release, and they are expected to be presented in a specific order. The following components should be found in all press releases:

1. **Statement on release time:** This statement should provide a date and time the information can be released to the public. For example, you can submit a press release on a Tuesday for information you do not want released until Friday.

2. **Contact information:** Directly below the release statement, you should provide full contact information for the person who should be contacted if further information is needed.

3. **Headline:** The headline should be a brief statement to get the attention of those reading it. It should be centered at the top of the page. Press releases with long, wordy, complicated, or boring headlines might be skipped over for more exciting news.

4. **Dateline:** Include in the dateline the date the press release is being submitted and the city, state, and country.

5. **Lead:** This opening paragraph should contain all the most basic and essential information. Answer the questions who, what, where, and when. This is the pertinent information that needs to be accurately relayed to the public.

6. **Body:** The second paragraph of the press release should answer the questions why and how. This paragraph will explain why the information in the first paragraph is newsworthy. However, the explanation should still be brief. A press release should be one page or less.

7. **Boilerplate:** This third and final paragraph in the press release should provide any additional information the media might be immediately interested in. The boilerplate paragraph should include a call to action.

8. **Call to action:** The call to action is a statement within the boilerplate paragraph that directs the media on what to do for more information. This can include an offer for an interview or an invitation to the event being announced.

9. **Closing:** Finish with a simple sign the press release is ending. This can be either the word END or the characters ###.

CASE STUDY: DEVELOPING A CAMPAIGN PLAN: AN OVERVIEW

Carol Hess
http://politicalresources.com
chess@politicalresources.com

The purpose of developing a campaign plan is to outline how you plan to get a 50 percent plus one majority on election day. Developing a campaign plan is crucial to your success. The plan is your road map to election day victory. It outlines each step in your campaign from the time you decide to run until the polls close on election day. Problems always arise, and campaign plans can be altered. What is important is that you have a plan outlining what you will do to win, how and when you will implement your strategy, and finally how much it will cost to do so.

Think about the following before you begin writing your plan:

1. Your campaign theme
2. The several issues you will run on
3. Events to highlight your issues
4. The profile of your election districts and the people and areas that are likely to vote for you

The next step is to determine how you will communicate your message to your people and get the 50 percent plus one majority.

You can communicate directly with voters by:
1. Going door to door
2. Writing to voters
3. Telephoning voters

You can communicate indirectly with voters with:
1. Yard signs and bumper stickers
2. Radio messages
3. Television messages
4. The Internet, both indirect and direct

To communicate your message, you need to raise money. Your campaign plan should outline the various forms of communication and the amount they will cost.

YOUR BASIC PLAN

	No. of Voters Reached	Campaign Timeline	No. of Volunteers	Costs
1. Direct voter contact				
a. Candidate door to door				
b. Outdoor events				
c. Volunteer door to door				
2. Direct mail				
a. Issue one				
b. Issue two				
c. Issue three				
d. GOTV				
3. Telephone				
a. Canvass - ID				
b. GOTV				
4. Radio				
a. Issue one				
b. Issue two				
c. Issue three				
d. GOTV				
5. Television				
a. Issue one				
b. Issue two				
6. Internet				
7. Yard signs and bumper stickers				

In addition, there should be cost estimates for office space, computer and other office equipment, and staff.

Once you have your written campaign plan, the next step is raise the funds to execute the plan.

Sources of money to fund the campaign:

1. Candidate
2. Family, friends, and associates
3. Candidate solicitation in person and by phone
4. Direct mail
5. Fundraising events
6. Other sources: PACs, the party

A well-thought-out plan will guide your campaign and can help raise money. You will have a good sense of the costs involved in communicating your message. This is important when approaching your family, friends, associates, or strangers. One of the first questions will certainly involve campaign costs. With an understanding of the campaign components, you can speak with greater authority and confidence.

Creating your Campaign Plan

Your campaign plan will be the guidebook for your entire campaign. You will create your campaign plan with your campaign manager and other trusted individuals. The campaign plan should include your strategy, goals, strengths, and weaknesses. It should also include an overview of your opponents' strengths and weaknesses. *This will be discussed further in Chapter 8.* Your campaign plan will contain a detailed timeline of your campaign, fundraising plans, donor lists, volunteer lists and resources, and a copy of your budget. Everything related to your campaign should be included in the campaign plan.

Keep your campaign plan close at hand. When questions about the direction of the campaign arise, refer to the campaign plan for guidance. Along with the goals of the campaign, the campaign plan should include the image you wish to put forward. This will include your slogan, logo, and sign design. Decide on and design any promotional material during the early stages of the campaign.

This is an essential part of the campaign because it will contain all the background research, goals, ideas, and timelines. When finished, the campaign plan will be the size of a book and be filled with written information, maps, and contact sheets. There should be only one copy of the campaign plan, and it should be guarded at all times. Having your opponent gain access to your campaign plan can be the end of your campaign. It will contain a lot of highly sensitive material. Allowing your opponent to read it would be the same as an NFL coach allowing the opposing team's coach to read the playbook.

The first section of the campaign plan should contain all the background research done before the election. You should include a copy of all the applicable election laws. Having them readily available will allow you to quickly answer questions that arise during the election. You should also include a written job description for the position in which you are seeking to be elected and a list of responsibilities. Next in this section, you should have a map of the district you would represent and the demographic information for the district. There should also be a description of the physical area and the voters in the area. Include a list of previous elections and the results, which should include voter turnout. Include a list of past issues within the district and the election results for those issues. How voters decide issues will provide insight into what is important to the them. Finally, add a list of specific issues that might have affected previous elections. For example, were there any political scandals during past elections or other problems that affected voter turnout?

The second section should focus on you and your opponent(s). First, include a detailed description of your experience, strengths, and weaknesses. Make a list of anything your opponent might be able to use against you within the realm of professionalism. Although these weaknesses might never come to light, you need to confront them yourself and be prepared to confront them publicly if you need to. Then, provide a full description of your opponent(s). This section will include all the information you gathered during your opponent research. *This topic will be addressed more fully in Chapter 8.*

The third section will address your specific goals during the campaign. Many local campaigns are won or lost by only a few votes. Know the numbers in your district. What is the total number of registered voters and the number of actual voters? To determine the number of actual voters, look at voter turnouts for the position for which you are running. Different positions often receive different turnout numbers. Once you determine the total voter turnout, determine how many votes you will need to win the election.

The fourth section will focus on where your target areas will be. *Targeting will be addressed more fully in Chapter 6.* For now, you should know that targeting involves determining which areas or groups of voters will be the source of the most swing votes. Start by making a list of the groups or areas within the district that have always voted for your party in your position. These basically are guaranteed votes. Unless they simply do not vote or you do something to greatly anger them, they are the voters who will vote for you without knowing much about you. Then, make a list of the groups or areas that have always voted for your opponents' party in this position. These are the votes you are unlikely to get no matter how much campaigning you do. The rest of the voters are the ones who either do not have a solid voting history or who have voted for either party in previous elections. These are the voters you want to identify and target during your campaign. To make the goals real, put this information in real numbers. For example, if 30 percent of the voters in the previous election are identified as swing voters, you need to determine how many actual people this accounts for. Are you looking at 30 percent of 300 or 30 percent of 30,000?

The fifth section of the campaign plan should be an outline of the key issues within the community. Which issues are important to the voters? These can include crime, schools, the local economy, the condition of the streets, or unemployment. Look at issues that have been voted on in previous elections and newspaper editorials to see what voters care about and what they are talking about. Once you have an exhaustive list of all issues, you will use this list to determine the political goals you will emphasize during the campaign.

The sixth section should be your official position on each of the issues. These should be thought about and written out in advance so you are prepared when questioned publicly. Each written response should be short, concise, and carefully crafted so your opponents or a member of the media cannot misquote or turn your statement around.

In the seventh section, you should include the official campaign message. This will be the statement released to the press and reiterated repeatedly throughout the campaign. This statement should answer the question, "Why are you running?" The campaign message should be thoughtful and concise. It should also take a stance and be decisive. Avoid generalizations, for example, that you want to help better schools. The campaign message should be a power statement, not a passive suggestion. The campaign message should also separate the candidate from their opponents. President Obama's 2008 campaign message was based on change because he knew people would relate the Republican candidate to the status quo, and he wanted to make sure people saw him as something different.

Using the campaign message in the previous section, the eighth section should contain the campaign's slogan and logo, your biography, and stories about your life that will support the campaign message. For example, if you are running on a family values platform, include messages about your children. If you endured or survived a hardship that will make you look stronger, prepare that story in advance so it is ready when needed. Any personal information about you that will strengthen your image or endear you to voters should be prepared in advance.

Section nine of the campaign plan should contain a detailed list of the intended campaigning strategies. This can include yard signs, commercials, booths at festivals and letters in the newspaper. Each idea should be written out with an approximate cost, relevant information, contacts, and timeline of when during the campaign the activity will take place.

Section 10 of the campaign plan should contain the campaign schedule. This will be a countdown to the election with all the campaign and fundraising activities and planned events and when they will be completed. Although items will be deleted and added to this list as needed, create a master schedule at the time the campaign plan is created.

Section 11 of the campaign plan should include a copy of the detailed campaign budget. Estimates for all expected costs should be collected and included in the budget before the start of the campaign. Not having a budget before the start of the campaign can quickly lead to a campaign disaster. Having a budget is essential to a smooth campaign.

Finally, in the last section of the campaign plan, include a list of every member of the campaign team. The list should include their position within the team, their responsibilities, and their complete contact information. This will make the information readily available if needed.

CASE STUDY: LOCAL POLITICIAN WHO RAN A SUCCESSFUL CAMPAIGN

David Taylor
Mayor
Amherst, Ohio

David Taylor has been a lifelong resident of Amherst, Ohio. After graduating from Amherst Central School, he attended Bowling Green State University. Taylor was elected twice to represent the second ward on the council. However, Taylor resigned this position to serve as safety service director for 10 years. After being unhappy with the way things were run, Taylor decided to put his years of political experience to work and run for mayor. Taylor won the position of mayor in 2004 and has held the position since.

While campaigning for the position of mayor, Taylor went door to door and used yard signs and direct mailings. He found benefit dinners to be the most useful way to raise funds for the campaign and make contact with his constituents. Taylor said the advantages of holding a political office include being able to serve the community and improve the conditions of the community. Taylor takes pride in improving services, completing projects within time and budget constraints, and serving the public. However, there are disadvantages to being an elected official. Sometimes he is forced to tell a constituent his or her request cannot be granted, and he knows he cannot please everyone he represents.

Taylor has found the experience of being an elected official rewarding, which is why he has dedicated so many years to service. Taylor advises aspiring politicians to avoid mudslinging and to always tell the truth. Additionally, Taylor asserts that having an extensive knowledge of the problems within the community and having ideas for possible solutions are essential for prospective candidates. Finally, candidates need to have solid communication skills, and they should never make promises they cannot keep.

Create a Timeline Counting Down to the Election

Most of the items discussed in Chapter 4 through Chapter 9 of this book will overlap or happen simultaneously. Creating a timeline of things that need to be accomplished between the start of the campaign and election day will help the campaign stay on track. The following sample timeline will help you to formulate your own timeline. Note that actual time frames will vary depending on the election laws and schedule in your area. Read local election laws and time frames before creating your campaign schedule.

SAMPLE TIMELINE

WEEK 21

o   Disaffiliate if you plan to run under an affiliation you are currently unable to.

WEEK 18

o   Pick the office for which you want to run.

o   Contact local party officials for the party you are affiliated with to let them know you plan to run. This is an important step to gain their support.

o   Get nomination petition forms from the board of elections.

o   Recruit volunteers to collect signatures.

o   Get monetary disclosure forms.

WEEK 17

o   Hire a campaign manager, volunteer coordinator, and treasurer.

o   Hold first staff meeting to create campaign plan.

o   Get maps of the voting district.

o   Start a database for volunteers, donors, and addresses.

o   Get professional photos taken for campaign literature.

WEEK 16

o   Have volunteer coordinator train and organize volunteers to collect signatures.

o   Begin collecting petition signatures.

o   Begin actively researching issues in the community and talking to residents.

WEEK 15

o   Hold a budget planning meeting.

o   Get estimates for printing literature and making signs.

o   Get estimates for all campaign costs, such as advertising and mailings.

o   Get estimates for all other costs, including stationary, copies, and handouts.

o   Consider all sources of incoming money, including your personal contribution, donations, and planned fundraisers.

WEEK 14

o   Sign up for speaking opportunities within the community.

WEEK 13

o   Make a master list of issues in the community.

o   Decide which issues are the most important.

o   Write your official position on each issue.

o   Select the one issue that will be the cornerstone of the campaign.

o   Choose a campaign theme and slogan.

WEEK 12

o   Design and write the campaign literature.

o   Design campaign letterhead.

o   Write a basic speech that will discuss the main campaign theme and slogan.

WEEK 11

o   Collect the nomination petition forms.

o   Go over each form to make sure they were completed correctly.

WEEK 10

- o   Submit the nomination petitions.

- o   Open a checking account for the campaign.

- o   Print the already designed campaign literature.

- o   Plan your announcement to run.

- o   Write a press release to the media announcing your plan to run for office.

WEEK 9

- o   Send a thank-you note to everyone who signed the petition along with an invitation to volunteer or attend a fundraising event.

WEEK 8

- o   Hold your initial fundraiser.

WEEK 7

- o   Hold an updated budget planning meeting now that money is beginning to come in from donors.

- o   If you plan to run radio ads, buy the radio time.

- o   Plan a candidate event for members of the community to meet the candidate.

- o   Have yard signs printed.

WEEK 6

- o   Begin having weekly staff meetings to keep everything on track.

- o   Have prominent supporters plan coffee gatherings; attend one each week until the election.

- o   Hold another candidate event or fundraiser.

- o   Making door-to-door visits to meet voters in the district.

WEEK 5

o   Buy newspaper space if you plan to use newspaper ads.

o   Continue visiting voters door to door.

o   Attend as many public meetings and functions as reasonably possible.

WEEK 4

o   Begin putting out yard signs.

o   Continue attending functions and coffee meetings and holding meet-the-candidate events.

WEEK 3

o   Hold a pep rally for all the volunteers.

o   Attend or organize a debate if possible.

o   Run first newspaper ad.

o   Review final budget.

WEEK 2

o   Take a day of rest during this week.

o   Send out bulk mailing to prospective voters.

o   Run second newspaper ad.

o   Run cable and radio spots.

WEEK 1

o   Mail second round of bulk mailing.

o   Schedule volunteers to hand out literature at the polls if allowed in your area.

o   Finish door-to-door visits.

o   Hold a staff meeting.

o   Hold a candidate event.

ELECTION DAY

- o Vote.

- o Have drivers available to drive people to the polls.

- o Provide food and drinks for volunteers working the polls.

Opening Your Campaign Headquarters

In small local elections, the campaign headquarters might be the candidate's house. However, renting a space in town will provide the public with a place to find information about the candidate and create a presence in the community. It will also provide a place for meetings, volunteer training sessions, and work days to complete tasks. In a large district, branch offices might also be needed in different areas of the district.

Your campaign headquarters should have regular business hours during which anyone can walk in off the street to volunteer or gain information. To ensure regular hours are kept, have one full-time person running the office. This will help maintain consistent operating hours. Your campaign headquarters should be kept clean at all times, and there should be plenty of regular activity there. This will make the place seem pleasant and approachable. Finally, either keep a script next to the phone for when people call or train a select number of people to answer the phone.

When the headquarters is ready to opened, the candidate can throw a grand opening party.

Your campaign headquarters should provide the following:

- A working bathroom
- Depending on the area and season, air conditioning
- Ample electrical outlets and phone jacks
- A clean work area
- Accessible parking
- Visible frontage for signs
- Security
- Good lighting
- A quiet area for meetings, research, and other intensive activities
- A central location in the voting district
- A convenient location for foot traffic
- A safe place to go to or leave from in the evening

The following materials and supplies are needed for a campaign headquarters run well:

Election-specific materials and supplies
- Alphabetized list of city streets
- Precinct maps
- Local phone books
- Multiple phones and phone lines
- List of polling locations
- Directory of volunteers and financial contributors
- City directory
- Copy of all applicable voting and election laws
- Voter registration locations and procedures
- At least one locking file cabinet to store sensitive information

General office supplies

- Desks
- Comfortable chairs
- Bookcases
- Filing cabinets
- Work tables
- Copy machine
- Large wall clock
- Bulletin boards
- Large wall calendar
- Trash bins
- Bins for recycling
- Tape
- File folders
- Address labels
- Pens
- Pencils
- Rubber bands
- Staplers and staples
- Index cards
- Sticky note pads
- Paper clips
- Calculator
- Poster board

Miscellaneous materials and supplies

- Refrigerator
- Coffee pot along with coffee, sugar, creamer, and artificial sweetener
- Coffee mugs

- Toilet paper
- Soap for the bathroom
- Broom and dustpan
- All-purpose cleaner and bathroom cleaner
- Paper towels
- Tissues
- Trash bags
- Television

Getting your Supporters in Line

The most important resource your campaign will have is its volunteers. Volunteers spread the word about your campaign and can convince others to vote for you. Even in small local elections, you cannot know everyone, so having a strong network of volunteers to spread your name will be beneficial. Volunteers are the backbone of any campaign. Recruiting volunteers and using them effectively is important. Your volunteer coordinator will need to be well-organized and a good listener. When volunteers are recruited, the coordinator should collect information from them to be able to contact them when needed. The following card is an example of a volunteer recruiting card, which should be used at the time the volunteer is recruited.

CITIZENS FOR _____

Name: _____

Address: _____

Home phone number: _____ Cell phone number: _____

I can help by donating: _____

I would like to help by:

_____making phone calls

_____sponsoring a coffee or brunch

_____putting up a yard sign

_____typing, mailing, and addressing envelopes

_____imputing data into the computer

_____researching online

_____distributing literature

_____driving and giving rides

_____registering voters

_____having the candidate speak to my group

_____other: _____

Your volunteers are an extension of you in the community. It is important to meet with your volunteers early in the process to let them know what your message is and how you want that message portrayed. If you are running against an unpopular opponent, you should describe how you want your volunteers to talk about that opponent in the public. You need to control the message while showing your volunteers how much you appreciate their support.

Setting Your Budget

Another indispensable aspect of your campaign structure is your budget. Money is key when running for office. Signs, buttons, and campaign posters all cost money. If you need to run television ads or radio spots, costs will increase. Although spending money is a necessity when running for political office, so is collecting money and properly showing where the collected money was spent. Any political campaign will require meticulous bookkeeping.

Political campaign funding and fraud are hot topics right now — in the minds of the government and those who oversee elections and in the minds of voters. By keeping updated financial records, you can quickly answer any questions that might arise about how you spent campaign money. By quickly answering these questions, you can dispel any thoughts of financial misbehavior.

By having a well-planned budget, you can also make the most of every dollar you bring in, which allows you to quickly respond to possible changes in the campaign. For example, suppose you have had success running ads on the radio, but your flier campaign is not seeing any returns. By thinking out your budget, you can quickly and easily move money around in your budget to make the best use of your resources.

Getting your Message Out

Chapter 6 will cover the ins and outs of actual campaigning, including producing campaign literature, gaining name recognition, and speaking to the voters. Before you can start actively campaigning, you will need to create your image. This will include choosing the name you want to be known by and the design of your signs. Many candidates chose to put their last name on their literature as a way to distinguish themselves from others who might have a similar or even the same name. For example, it would not be wise to simply run on the name Bill. It is too common. However, some people want to separate themselves from the public's associations of their last name. For example, when Hillary Clinton ran for Senate, her signs, banners, and ads displayed only her first name. Some candidates run on nicknames because it makes them more personable to the public. Still, other candidates run on their first name to promote the idea they are part of the community. Congressman Dennis Kucinich from Cleveland displays only his first name on his signs.

In addition to the sign display, it is also important to create a campaign slogan during this period. Although campaign slogans are not always necessary, they can help identify a candidate during an intense campaign. Candidates should also get promotional pictures taken early on in the process. These pictures will be used on all the promotional material and campaign literature. Candidates should be dressed appropriately for the setting of the photo. For example, if the candidate is visiting a construction site, he or she should be wearing a hard hat. The following is a list of suggested photos to have taken and use during the campaign:

- Professional head shot
- Candidate leading a meeting in a business suit
- Candidate in a public park during a cleanup or tree planting
- Candidate with his or her family

- Candidate sitting a table with an elderly couple
- Candidate speaking publicly
- Candidate at a desk working
- Candidate speaking with veterans
- Candidate in uniform if he or she is former military, police, or firefighter
- Candidate at a rally or surrounded by supporters

Taking a large number of photos will allow the candidate to choose the photos he or she feels best suits his or her goals. These photos can be used in a variety of different ways and will project the image the candidate wants people to see. It is also important the candidate maintain the same physical appearance as seen in the campaign literature. The candidate should not lose or gain noticeable weight, change hairstyles, or decide to grow facial hair. If a candidate is trying to build name recognition, he or she will only confuse voters by changing appearances during the campaign.

Creating Campaign Literature

Once the pictures are taken, it is time to design and create the campaign literature. The campaign literature will include yard signs, fliers or postcards to be sent through the mail, door hangers or cards to leave during the door-to-door canvasses, and brochures or postcards to distribute while talking to potential voters. Each of these items should be professionally printed. Although you might be capable of making them at home, it is not a wise area in which to cut costs. If the campaign literature does not look professional, voters will see it as a reflection of you as a candidate.

The campaign literature should feature a photo of you and a brief description of your qualifications, your campaign message, or other concise and easy-to-read text. The written information on the campaign literature should be limited. If the literature has too many words, most people will not stop to read it. The text should also be large. Photos, logos, or familiar icons can also be used on campaign literature.

All visual information should be consistent. For example, the font used to write the candidate's name should be the same on every piece of literature. The way in which the name is written should also be the same. Females should never switch between a married name and a maiden name during a campaign. This will confuse voters. Additionally, once a logo and slogan are decided on, it should not be changed. It will be a sign of inconsistency and indecision on the part of the candidate.

Many candidates like to distribute other items, such as cups, hats, nail files, or yard sticks with their name and information on them. There is much debate over whether these items help get votes. Whether these items are ordered should be based on the available budget. However, if possible, all volunteers should be provided with campaign shirts to wear at campaign events and rallies. For lesser-known candidates, extra items can help build name recognition.

Preparing for the Next Step

The next step in your campaign is to ensure you have a working budget and a plan to cover expenses. Although this process will begin simultaneously with the other actions mentioned in this chapter, it is an important and detailed process that should be addressed separately. Before turning your attention to fundraising efforts and finances, make sure you are fully prepared to move forward. The following checklist will guide you through the process of starting your campaign.

☑ CHAPTER CHECKLIST

☐ Collect copies of all the election laws that apply to the position for which you intend to run.

☐ Pick up all needed forms from the clerk's office, including the nomination petitions and monetary disclosure forms.

☐ Collect nomination signatures.

☐ Read and fill out monetary disclosure forms.

☐ Meet with your core team and create your campaign plan.

☐ Have your volunteer coordinator begin organizing and recruiting volunteers.

☐ Create the design for your signs.

☐ Create your slogan if you chose to have one.

☐ Have professional photos taken to use during your campaign.

CHAPTER 5

Never Underestimate the Importance of Money

The American political system is set up to allow anyone who is qualified to run for political office — despite what some cynics might say. No office is off-limits to the constituents it serves based on their wealth. Still, money is a key component to any campaign. You cannot underestimate the importance of money in your campaign. Money buys advertisements, services, and supplies. Although money is important in a campaign, there are many ways to get money if you personally do not have a lot of it. Many campaigns run on donations, which makes fundraising events a central part of the campaign.

In addition to raising and spending money, simply tracking the money and appropriately planning how it will be spent are vitally important functions. One of the first things you need to do when planning your campaign is create a campaign budget. The budget can be adjusted throughout the campaign as different decisions are made, but there should be an initial budget to use as a guiding force. The initial budget will also provide a realistic view of what the candidate will need to raise to campaign in the way he or she wants. Otherwise, the candidate will need to cut back on the expenses of campaigning and try a more grassroots approach.

Know the Law

Fundraising and political campaign contributions have been brought to the forefront in recent years, especially when John Mc-Cain ran for re-election. The Bipartisan Campaign Reform Act of 2002, or the McCain-Feingold bill, which Congress passed in 2002, sought to limit the amount of funds that could be contributed to campaigns through certain organizations. Due to the popularity and media coverage of the proposal, voters and officials are much more aware of candidate fundraising tactics than ever before. This puts candidates and fundraisers in position to raise as much money as they can while still showing they are following the rules.

The first thing you want to do when beginning to raise money is to know the law. States and local municipalities might have laws defining how much you can raise, how much certain individuals can give, and how those funds can be raised. Work with your county or city clerk's office to learn all the rules that affect your area so if a question arises about impropriety in your fundraising tactics, you have a solid legal background to fall back on.

In addition, always be upfront with your fundraising tactics and never attempt to hide anything from the public. Sometimes tactics are legally sound, but if they are done in a way that raises doubt in the public's mind, those tactics can still be detrimental to your campaign. However, the public might view that same tactic as acceptable if done up front with full disclosure. What the voters are looking for are signs of deceit, and if you show you are honest and up front, you will put forth a trustworthy image.

It is best to obtain a written copy of all the laws pertaining to your campaign. This will help you avoid the mistake of believing someone else's interpretation of the law, which might be wrong. Violating election laws can quickly result in being disqualified as a candidate. Once a candidate is disqualified, all the time, money, and resources already invested into the campaign are lost.

Creating a Budget

Creating a budget is a necessary process. The first step to setting a budget is to brainstorm two lists. The first list will contain all the necessary items. This list will include stationary, envelopes, postage, printing services for brochures, yard signs, phone service, access to a computer and copier and district maps. The second list will contain optional things you will get if you can afford them. This list might include hats, T-shirts, buttons, pencils, and other promotional items. This second list might also include radio and cable ads, newspaper ads, and other means of advertising. These items will improve your campaign by increasing your name recognition, but they can be cut down or eliminated if the budget does not allow for them.

The next step is to get estimates for everything on both lists. Find out whether you can get any of the items free or donated, and then make a list of prices for anything you will need to spend money on, such as postage and yard signs. Once you have a complete list of expenses, you will have an idea of how much money you need to contribute or raise to have a successful campaign. For example, if your total expenses equal $10,000 and you only have $5,000 to personally invest, you need to be prepared to raise another $5,000.

Once you know how much money you need to raise, create a plan with your fundraising coordinator. This plan needs to include a list of a variety of low-cost fundraising ideas with realistic expectations for how much money can be raised. You cannot assume one big event will raise all the money needed for the election or a simple appeal for donations will do the trick. Plan events that will raise more than you need in case any of the events fall short of expectations. If you raise more than expected, you can splurge on a campaign item you did not think you could afford.

Sample budget

As your campaign progresses, you can make adjustments in your spending. For example, in the following sample budget, the amount of money raised is clearly higher than the amount of money being spent. The candidate might choose to increase their commercials during the last weeks of the campaign or do an additional mailing. Likewise, if the campaign does not raise as much as expected, the candidate should cut spending.

	June	July	August	September	October
Phones	$300	$300	$300	$300	$300
Phone deposit	$1,000				
Supplies	$100	$100	$100	$100	$100
Postage	$50	$50	$50	$200	$300
Volunteer expenses	$100	$100	$200	$200	$300
Printing					
Fliers	$100		$100		$300
Pamphlets				$250	$250
Yard signs, buttons, etc.				$500	
Fundraising expenses	$1,500	$100	$1,000	$100	$2,000
Direct mail				$1,000	$1,000
Volunteer canvass				$250	$500
Radio					$1,000
Television					$5,000
GOTV					$2,000
Total Expenses	**$3,150**	**$650**	**$1,750**	**$2,900**	**$13,500**
Contributions					
Candidate			$2,000	$2,000	$2,000
Local political party				$500	$500
Fundraising efforts	$13,500	$1,000	$4,500	$1,200	$8,000
Total Income	**$13,500**	**$1,000**	**$6,500**	**$3,700**	**$10,500**
Monthly difference	**+$10,350**	**+$350**	**+$4750**	**+$800**	**-$3000**

Private Funds

· ·

The easiest way to fund your campaign is through your own private funds. Private funds are your own money, and most places do not have laws limiting how much of your own money you can throw into your election campaign. Although this is the easiest way to finance your campaign, you need to weigh the pros and cons of using your own money. Funding a campaign with personal money eliminates the need to hold fundraising events and solicit donations, which is something many people are not comfortable doing. It might also endear the candidate to many prospective voters who like candidates who do not ask for money.

Personal investments can be risky

You will likely spend some of your own money in the course of your campaign. How much you spend is the key. For most local elections, a modest amount of money must be used to get the ball rolling, but fundraising should pick up the rest. This might be the answer if a candidate does not have a lot of personal money to spend.

For other more high-profile elections, candidates can spend tens or hundreds of thousands of dollars or more of their own money. The amount of your own money you spend might say a lot to your voters. Like any campaign financing, what you spend on yourself is open for public review. The voting public can see exactly how much you put into your campaign.

This can help or hurt you. If you live in a poorer rural area and the voters see you are putting a lot of money into your campaign, you might unwittingly disconnect with your constituents. They might look at you as just another well-off politician. Again, this is where knowing your community and your constituents can help you make a good decision about how you portray yourself.

Another aspect of using your own funds that might be unappealing is the return on investment. There is no guarantee you will win the election. Without winning, you might have nothing to show for the money you spent. Consider how much the office you are running for pays and how much power you will have. You might not want to overdo personal spending if the office you are running for does not pay much or does not have as much power as the amount you spent would warrant.

Fundraising

The number one way to raise money for a campaign is through fundraising. Fundraising includes events and ongoing solicitation of donations from individuals and businesses. Fundraising is a tool used in every campaign all the way up to the presidential elections. Fundraising events also provide candidates with an opportunity to meet their potential voters. In essence, fundraising is simply asking your supporters for money. For most people, this goes against what they have been taught as children: that it is not acceptable to beg for money. For candidates, asking for money is often essential.

At the beginning of your campaign you will need to create a fundraising plan in addition to your budget. This should include a list of fundraising activities and the estimated amount each activity will earn. Once they have been decided on, the fundraising coordinator will then organize and carry out each activity. If you are running in a voting district that varies in socioeconomic status, it is important to hold both large and small fundraising events that even those without a lot to donate can attend. Holding only high-priced dinners will alienate those who cannot afford to attend.

Know your audience

How do you raise funds? The first step is to know your audience. Often, fundraisers are gatherings of supporters, but other times, they involve direct solicitation with supporters asking others for financial backing. For example, if there is a country club in your area with many possible supporters who are influential, holding a golf outing might produce good results. If you live in a family-oriented community, consider holding a family fun day or a carnival. Just be sure to target your audience, and do not spend more than you think you can bring in with the fundraiser.

Know what the people you are asking money from are looking for in their candidate. If they are supporters, they want to know that you are still energetic, committed to your message, and ready to take their local government where they want it to go. If they are people in the general public who might not have made a decision on who they will vote for, they want to know you are listening to them and will be a trustworthy representative in their government.

Types of fundraisers

Part of knowing your audience is knowing which types of fundraisers to hold. The number of fundraising ideas you can use for an election is endless. The best fundraisers are ones that get your supporters together to encourage enthusiasm for the race and allow people to get to know the candidate better. Voters need to feel local candidates care about their problems. Although elected officials cannot solve every problem, they can show the people they care and are doing their best. Fundraising events are opportunities to show voters you care.

Appeal for donations

One way to raise money without spending a lot is to simply ask people for donations. Ask family and friends for donations toward your campaign. Get a list of donors who have contributed to previous campaigns for your position or political party. Contact them directly, and tell them exactly why you are the perfect person for the job and why they should support you. Contact local businesses and ask for their support. When the volunteer coordinator requests volunteers, have him or her ask every person whether he or she would like to make a donation. Many people would like to help with political campaigns, but they simply do not have the time. Donating money allows them to feel they have helped in some way.

While soliciting donations, keep a detailed record of donors, their contact information, and the amount of their donation. This information is important because it helps you complete the monetary disclosure forms, which you will be required to submit throughout the race, and it allows you to send personal thank-you cards. Send one card immediately after the donation is made, and send a second card after you win the election to thank them again for their generous support. People generally like to be thanked and feel appreciated for the things they do. This will also make them more likely to donate to future campaigns.

Name	Address	City	ZIP code	Phone Number	Amount	1st Thank You Sent	2nd Thank You Sent
Bill Smith	123 Street	Elyria	44035	123-456-7890	$100	X	
Wendi Black	123 Road	Elyria	44035	123-456-7890	$200	X	
Barb Stasiuk	123 Trail	Elyria	44035	123-456-7890	$50	X	

Door-to-door canvassing

Going door to door can be one of the best types of fundraisers for local elections because of what you can accomplish in the process of raising funds. With a smaller geographic area, you can reach more of your possible constituents, and in addition to raising money for your campaign, you can spread your message in the community. In small local elections, have the people who are helping you raise money talk about the message first before asking for a donation. If the voter believes in what you or your volunteers are saying, he or she might be more willing to give money to your cause.

This is also a good time to poll the neighborhoods you go into. While at the door, volunteers can gauge whether a certain area is pulling for you or whether the citizens of that area are undecided. This can help you better understand where to place your advertisements and how to spend the money you have raised.

Also re-affirm or discover which new issues are on people's minds for the upcoming elections. Volunteers can poll individuals on which issues are key to them in the upcoming election or in the city in general. If a certain issue keeps coming up, it might be a growing topic people are talking about. If you find out about it first, you could have an edge. If you begin talking about the issue before your opponent, you will appear to be someone who is in touch with the people.

Dinners

Hosting a dinner is another popular type of fundraiser. Used a lot on the state and national level, a fundraising dinner can be a way to raise some needed funds for your campaign. With this type of fundraiser, the candidate hosts the dinner and charges a set amount per plate. The night consists of speeches and reaffirmations of your message and stance on important issues. Because supporters attend the dinner, you can rally those who are behind you. Most attendees will be glad to pay the charge per plate because they already know you hold the same values.

One of the primary benefits of holding dinners is the candidate knows the minimum he or she will raise if all the seats are sold. Limiting the number of tickets will create a sense of urgency. If tickets are limited to 200 and sold for $100 each, which is not unreasonable for this type of event, the candidate knows he or she will raise $20,000 in addition to the money people donate while at the dinner. Fundraising dinners for state and federal candidates often cost more than $1,000 per ticket. To keep the costs of the dinner as minimal as possible, the fundraising coordinator should approach individuals and businesses that support the candidate to help host the event and donate services and resources to make it successful. For example, in July 2008, Warren Buffet, who was a strong supporter of President Obama during his campaign, headlined a fundraising dinner that cost $28,500 per person. It was held at the home of Penny Pritzker, Obama's finance chair, and his senior adviser, Valerie Jarrett, hosted it.

Planning a fundraising event

A successful fundraising event starts with research. Look into the types of fundraising events that have been successful in your area in the past. Also research the types of marketing and advertising used during previous successful fundraising events. The more information you have before planning a fundraising event, the better the chances are your event will be successful. Determine the types of events that will be successful in your area and the amount of money you can charge for tickets.

When planning a fundraising dinner event, choose a theme. The theme should cater to the area if possible. Some themes that might be popular include a wine tasting; Mardi Gras; or an era, such as the 1920s or 1940s. When choosing a theme, be creative and think of something that will allow for a fun atmosphere. You want those who attend to be able to relax and have a good time.

Check the community calendar to choose a date that will not conflict with other important community events. Once you determine a date, choose a location for the event. The location should be suitable for the theme. For example, if you are having a wine-tasting event, hold the fundraiser at a local winery. If you are throwing a 1920s-themed party, rent a hall with a large dance floor and recreate the feel of a speak-easy.

Two issues to carefully consider to have a successful fundraiser are manpower and budget. You will want to use volunteers to reduce the costs of the event. Without an adequate number of volunteers, it might be difficult to accomplish everything on time and still allow for a smooth evening. Budget is also a major concern. Do not overspend on a fundraising event. All money spent takes away from the total amount of money earned.

When determining the budget for the event, obtain estimates for all possible expenses, including the venue, entertainers, decorations, food, supplies, printing, and advertising. The best way to host a large event and keep costs down is to solicit donations of supplies and services from local businesses. You can also get local businesses to sponsor the event to help defer costs.

Once you determine the date, time, and location, use an extensive checklist to ensure everything is taken care of. Similar to a wedding, a large event, such as a fundraising dinner, involves multiple tasks that need to be completed simultaneously.

The following checklist can get you started, but it should be tailored to the specific size and theme of your event. The timeline should go backward from the day of the event. The to-do list for the day of the event should be broken down by the hour.

- ❑ Entertainment
- ❑ Food
- ❑ Dessert

- ☐ Wait staff

- ☐ Table decorations

- ☐ Hall decorations

- ☐ Advertising for the event

- ☐ Ticket sales

- ☐ Reservations

- ☐ Ticket printing

- ☐ Event set up

- ☐ Event clean up

- ☐ Timeline of activities during the event

- ☐ Speakers

- ☐ Activities, such as dancing and door prizes

- ☐ Security

- ☐ Press releases sent to all local media outlets

- ☐ Post-event evaluation

- ☐ Team meeting

Other events

Most events can be made into a fundraiser. Depending on what is popular in your area, consider planning a dance, silent auction, golf outing, steak fry, rib festival, or chili cook-off. If something is unique to your area, play it up. Not only can you raise some funds, but you will show you are connected with the area and its customs. Voters like candidates who act as one of them. Also, by thinking creatively, you show your future constituents you are not like other candidates and can bring a fresh approach to issues and government. Organizing and attending less formal events will also show voters you are a normal person who likes to have fun. You do not want to appear stiff or unapproachable.

Other fundraising event ideas include:

- Golf tournament
- Poker tournament
- Las Vegas night
- Wine tasting
- Art raffle
- Dinner theater
- Breakfast
- Comedy night
- Night at the races
- Night of dancing or throwback prom
- Karaoke
- Family events, such as a cookout or skating party
- Meet-and-greets or coffee socials
- Auction for an experience
- Online fundraisers through candidate's website

- Money bomb (set a real goal and challenge supporters to donate money on a designated day to reach the goal within 24 hours)

Tying the fundraiser to your message

No matter which fundraiser you choose to employ, you need to make a point of relating the event to your message. As with events styled after meet-and-greets, putting a spin on your fundraising efforts that reinforces your message can help put you and your message more in the minds of the voters. Never lose sight of your purpose or reason for planning the event. You want people to vote for you, and to do that, they need to know what you are going to do for the community.

If you run on a family-based platform, a dinner that is family-friendly or a cookout can be a way to raise money. Also, a mini-carnival with a few fun games for children to play could boost your standing in the community. If you are running on a business platform, hosting a formal dinner and inviting business leaders to attend is the perfect venue in which to discuss your business policies. Whatever your message, tying it to your fundraising efforts will make people feel less as though they are giving money to an individual instead of a cause they believe in — and that can help mobilize your supporters.

Vary your fundraising efforts

Vary the types of fundraisers you use to make sure you reach the maximum number of people and appear as a candidate everyone can support. If the only fundraiser you hold is a dinner for local business leaders, the general public might take that to mean you are in the pocket of the business class. On the other hand, if you hold family-style fundraisers or off-the-wall fundraisers, people might not take you as seriously as you would like them to.

Being a candidate for political office requires you to constantly balance different aspects of your campaign. A candidate needs to be strong and confident and be someone who listens to and represents the people. At the same time, the candidate must also be a strong advocate for business. Offer a wide variety of events and opportunities for voters to meet you and donate their money or volunteer their time. The more people you let into your circle of supporters, the more votes you will get from supporters and from their family and friends. Word-of-mouth promotion is still one of the best means of getting your name out.

Public Funds

Every year, a certain amount of tax money is set aside for use in elections. These are called public funds, and they exist to help anyone run for office no matter what their fiscal situation is. Anyone can use these public funds, but some strings are attached.

Check availability

The first thing you want to do when considering using public funds for your campaign is find out how much is available to you. Different areas have different rules about how much money can be used to fund campaigns, so be sure to check with your local, state, and even the federal government to find out whether money is available for you. This will help you determine how much money you will have so you can set up your budget properly and make the best use of the money you have coming in.

Public fund laws

Using public funds does make a candidate more susceptible to laws governing the use of those funds. Money received from the public coffers rarely comes with no strings attached, so be wary of what those laws are and how they will hinder or help your campaign.

Using public funds can be an option for those who start out with limited finances, but in some areas, rules are in place for how much you can raise on your own outside the public funds you receive and how much you can contribute yourself. You want to weigh the amount you would get from the public fund against how much you could raise if left to your own efforts. It might not make sense for you to bind yourself if the laws in your area put a limit on how much you can raise and you have a wealthy support base.

Hitting the Campaign Trail

The processes of setting a budget and raising funds are important aspects of the election process but are still just parts of the bigger campaign. *Chapter 6 will further discuss the act of campaigning.* First, review the following checklist to make sure you have taken care of everything regarding your budget and fundraising efforts.

☑ CHAPTER CHECKLIST

❏ Investigate election laws for budgets and donations.

❏ Create a list of expenses, and gather estimates of cost.

❏ Create a list of revenue sources.

❏ Develop a fundraising plan based on the amount of money needed.

❏ Initiate your fundraising plan, and follow through until the needed funds are raised.

❏ Investigate the availability of public funds.

❏ Send thank-you cards to all donors.

CHAPTER 6

On the Campaign Trail

· ·

For most candidates in local elections, hitting the campaign trail is their first taste of politics. This is the time when you start talking to voters and spreading your message. It is also the time when you begin meeting the other individuals who will shape your political career, including current politicians, business leaders, and in some cases, party representatives.

How you interact with all these groups will determine your success during the campaign and during your term in office and beyond. The ties you build now on the campaign trail will stay with you throughout your career. Your ability to present yourself and motivate others will make a big difference on election day. Campaigning is your chance to build name recognition and deliver your message to the voters.

Reaching the Constituents

Putting your face on a billboard with a message that says "vote for me" will get you face recognition, but it might not get the voters to rally to your cause. Voters want to hear your voice or at least hear you answer some of their questions. Still, name recognition is vital. If voters cannot remember your name, they will not know who to vote for on election day.

Many opportunities to meet your constituents in person or have your message spread among a wide audience will come up. Always keep your message fluid. When you meet with the public, listen to their concerns and adjust the tone of your message accordingly. Taking advantage of each of the following events and forums will pay off on election day, but address each in a different manner.

The town hall meeting

Town hall meetings have lately become more popular on the national stage. Senators, congressional representatives, and even presidential candidates are using the events to boost voter approval and get in front of the people. However, town hall meetings have long been a staple of the local election circuit, so mastering these events will be important to winning the election.

The town hall meeting format is more laid back than other events at which candidates will speak to the public directly. In its purest sense, anyone in the "town" can come and ask questions to a candidate during a this type of meeting. Most town hall meetings today come with guidelines and time limits for questions and responses, but the spirit of the town hall meeting is still intact, especially at the local level. Area constituents will come in and ask questions of you to see whether your views are in line with theirs. For local politicians with relatively small constituencies, these town hall meetings will be important because many, if not most, of the voters who will be going to the polls could be at the meeting.

The town hall meeting format can be a tricky one for candidates. Because questions are random, the candidate needs to be able to answer questions on the fly. Anyone can ask a question at a town meeting. To be successful at a town hall meeting, you must do a couple of things. First, know your message. What issues are you running on? What needs to change and what needs to stay the same? If you know these answers, you can tailor your responses to meet the goals you set for your candidacy and can better react when a question catches you off guard.

Second, keep a level head. Crowds can often be emotional. Leaders are not ruled by emotions, so although some emotion is good, too much emotion can be viewed as a sign of weakness. Think of Howard Dean, one of the presidential candidates in the 2004 election, and his outburst when he was caught yelling like a madman during a rally. At the time, he was the front-runner for the Democratic nomination, but after his outburst, his following fell off dramatically. If you can keep a level head, demonstrate that the concerns of the public are your concerns, and answer the questions in a professional manner, you can relay to the crowd you are ready to be a leader. Your opponent will likely attempt to get you angry and worked up by attacking your ability to perform the job; brush off these attacks and focus on your message.

Local debates

Local debates are in some ways easier to handle than town hall meetings, but in other ways, they are more challenging. They are easier because a moderator is likely to stick to certain subjects, which is unlike the town hall meeting during which the questions could be related to a variety of topics. You can prepare your answers. But the debate is more difficult because your opponent is also well-prepared and you must interact with your opponent on the answers. Like in a town hall meeting, it is important to come prepared and with good knowledge of what your message is and what your campaign stands for.

Debates are more formal than town hall meetings. Two candidates answer the same questions that deal directly with the main issues of the campaign. With a moderator asking the questions, there is little chance for surprise or for emotional questions to arise. Moderators are there to provide questions with no bias, but at a town hall meeting, the person asking the question might be on your opponent's side and trying to trap you. The format follows a pattern of answer, rebuttal, and second rebuttal pattern. The candidate who answers first switches every question.

The debate is more of a head-to-head contest between candidates. The candidate who sounds the most professional and has what the public thinks are the best answers will win the debate. The debate format allows a candidate to practice answering questions about topics that are most likely going to be brought up. This can give you an edge if you are well prepared and your opponent is not.

Although media outlets sometimes call a winner of a debate, most of the voting public does not truly know what that means. To be successful as a debater in a local election, you have to know what the issues are and ways to fix them, have the concerns of the voters at heart, and convince voters you will not let them down if elected to office. The outcomes of debates in local elections can have a big impact on where the vote goes if both candidates have done a good job getting their name out to voters, so preparing and doing well in a debate will be key to your success. Look the part of a leader: Dress nicely; speak with a firm, confident voice; and stay true to the message of your campaign. These can all help you come out ahead in this crucial part of any campaign.

SAMPLE DEBATE QUESTIONS

1. How will your experience help you in the position of _____?

2. What changes do you feel would improve the school proficiency exams?

3. Unemployment in our area is at an all-time high. What do you plan to do to promote jobs?

4. What would attract more businesses to this area?

5. How do you feel about extending the public nonsmoking laws to this area?

6. During the past year, three police officers have been laid off, how do you plan to ensure the city is protected?

7. Along with the unemployment rate, the rate of homelessness within our city has also risen. Which programs do you feel should be initiated to help those in need?

8. Where do you stand on the sudden increase in local gambling facilities in our area?

9. The previous administration ran our city into a $50,000 deficit. What do you plan to do to rectify that?

10. How do you plan to improve communication between the city council and the mayor's office?

11. What are your short- and long-term goals if elected?

12. What new ideas do you plan to bring to the table to alter the status quo?

13. Since the hospital moved out of the city, the building has stood empty in a prime part of town. What do you think should be done to effectively use that space?

How to prepare for a debate

To prepare for a debate, have every member of your team think of possible questions and write them on index cards. Get transcripts or tapes of previous debates, and write down all the questions asked during those debates. Once you have all the questions written on individual index cards, go through the questions one at a time and create answers for them. Have several statements prepared in your head that will redirect a question or attack to your campaign message.

Well in advance of the debate, chose the outfit you are going to wear. Making a last-minute decision or changing your mind at the last minute can throw you off mentally and affect your temperament during the debate. Have the outfit you plan to wear dry-cleaned and set aside for the day of the debate. Avoid planning any other events on the day of the debate. You want to focus on staying calm and prepared that day.

As the debate approaches, have a mock debate with your team. Invite volunteers to be in the audience. Have one team member act as your opposition and another team member act as the moderator. Have the moderator ask questions at random so you do not know what will be asked when. This will force you to remember the answers you prepared on the spot. Have the mock debate videotaped so you can watch yourself afterward. Ask your volunteer audience for their honest opinions on how you did.

Newspapers

Newspaper readership has declined in recent years, but do not underestimate this medium, especially when it comes to local elections. Small-town or rural voters will often have few options when it comes to finding out about local government, so a local newspaper might be how they get their news. Consequently, local newspapers are a way to reach them and the people they talk to about the local elections.

The news a newspaper produce is written by someone other than you. You might give an hour-long interview with a newspaper, but you can't control which quotes and comments make it into the story. Radio or television news coverage of the election might do the same thing, but you can also purchase advertising time to get your face, and message, across to viewers and listeners. In a newspaper, ad space is two-dimensional, and what you say is limited to a few lines because newspapers charge per inch of space.

How do you work with newspapers at the local level? Be accessible. The news is supposed to be unbiased, but if a newspaper reporter likes you and believes in your message, she might be a little more sympathetic than if she did not like you. Treat the newspaper reporter as a possible voter, and use the time you spend with him as a way to hone your communication skills. However, always keep in mind a reporter is not your friend. Avoid getting too personal. If you do, you might say something you will regret seeing in the paper the next day.

By being accessible, you can also build a comfort level with the newspaper, so if a last-minute issue comes up before press time, the newspaper will call you or your campaign for comment rather than your opponent. This means you will be quoted in the story everyone is reading while your opponent might be listed as unavailable for comment, and no one wants a leader who is unavailable. Your public relations specialist will work for you to maintain an open and positive relationship with the local newspapers if that is possible.

Radio

Radio ads will get your message out, especially if you are in a tightly contested campaign. It is hard to go through a day without hearing something on the radio whether at work, in the car, or at the gym; at some point, you hear what is happening on the radio. Another way to get your voice on the radio is by being interviewed. In many situations, radio hosts enjoy the opportunity to talk to candidates on air. However, be prepared. Taking this approach means you will be live on the air, and you cannot control what the radio host will ask you.

Taking out a spot on a local radio station can be a way to reach voters in your area. Although the ads cost more than newspaper ads, for example some stations can charge up to $1,000 per one-minute ad, you can reach more people. It also allows you to tailor your message to who is listening to the station. Radio comes in several genres, and each radio station sticks to its specific niche. For example, sports radio talks about sports, and news channels talk about news. The audiences who listen to those stations also often have common general characteristics. This allows you to tweak your message so you can maximize the results from each particular audience instead of reaching a wide sampling of voters who are watching television or reading newspapers.

With radio ads, you also have complete control of the message. People only hear what your ad says. You get a 30-second or one-minute spot to deliver your message, which is a good length of time to talk to potential supporters.

Television

Television ads are the most expensive option for getting your message out, but they can also have the most impact. Television ads can cost between $1,000 and $350,000 depending on the quality of your ad. However, television gives you the opportunity to show people your name and appearance simultaneously while they hear you reiterate your message. Although viewers have likely heard or read your message through other media, hearing you personally say it makes a difference.

Television ads are a little riskier for delivering your message. As easily as a good television advertisement can sway people, an advertisement that does not appropriately relay your message can be a detriment. Unlike other types of ads in which you are only using one sense, television combines sight, sound, and reading. That means your message must be on target, your body language must be clear and professional, and the text on the screen must be accurate and easy to read. Because there is so much room for error combined with a potentially large impact, you need to make sure your television commercial is produced well.

When dealing with television ads, know your constituents and their prevailing feeling on the issues at the heart of the election. You do not want to run a television ad that takes a stance on an issue only to find out most of the voting public does not agree with your opinion.

Appearance is another factor. Not only will the viewers hear your message, they will see what you look like and how you carry yourself. Your physical appearance should be similar to your appearance in your campaign literature. Getting a drastic haircut or changing the look of facial hair can lead to confusion and voter distrust. Voters should be able to recognize you on the street based on your ads. Viewers will judge you on the many nonverbal messages your body sends out. When shooting or approving a television ad, consider which nonverbal cues you are sending.

Television ads are not for everyone. In races for city government or county positions, television ads might be necessary. For smaller government positions, a television ad might be too costly for the amount of people it would reach. With any type of advertisement, always weigh benefits and downfalls of the medium before purchasing the ad space. If there are better or cheaper ways of reaching your intended audience, try them before spending the money on a television ad.

Yard signs

Yard signs are an important aspect of campaigning because they accomplish two things.

First, yard signs help build name recognition. Potential voters will see your name repeatedly. Even if they do not know much about you, they might vote for you on election day simply because they recognize your name on the ballot. Name recognition is one of the primary advantages incumbents have. Yard signs also show the public how many people support you. Yard signs, as the name suggests, are displayed in the front yards of your supporters. If an undecided voter drives through town and sees dozens of signs with your name on them, he or she will be more inclined to vote for you simply because it appears that everyone else is.

Distributing yard signs is also a way to talk to people through door-to-door campaigning. If you or a volunteer visit citizens at their home and ask to put a sign in their yard, they will likely want to know more about you. That allows you or one of your volunteers to briefly introduce you and your message. Distributing yard signs is one of the many jobs volunteers can do. It would be impossible for a single candidate to canvass an entire community unless he or she lived in a small community.

Meet-and-greets

Advertisements in newspapers, on the radio, or on television are good because you can control the message and reach a wide range of people. However, they do not provide the personal contact with voters a town hall meeting or a debate does. Although paid advertisements will help you build name recognition, they will not endear you to the public.

A way to combine the two is with a meet-and-greet. During a meet-and-greet, you host an event open to the public at which citizens can come in and meet with you. Meet-and-greets are informal and have no set question-and-answer time, but they allow people to come and go, shake hands with you, and get to know you a little bit more.

Light snacks and refreshments are always a good idea at these events. A common meet-and-greet is a coffee social. These can be held in community halls or hosted in the home of a strong supporter. Meet-and-greets are a way to show off your personal side. Voters are more likely to vote for someone they know, trust, and have a personal bond with at least on some level. Meet-and-greets, though, are not as easy as they sound, and you need to avoid the pitfalls that can come with an informal meeting with the public. By assessing the areas you excel at, you can determine whether a meet-and-greet is right for your campaign.

Assessing your social skills

Hosting a meet-and-greet requires a candidate with good social skills. Can you strike up a conversation with just about anyone? Can you talk on any topic? Do people feel comfortable talking to you? If you said yes to any of these, a meet-and-greet is a good opportunity to let people know who you are. If you answered no to any of these questions, you should go back to Chapter 2 and ask yourself whether political office is the right vocation for you.

Conversely, if you do not do well in large groups, cannot work a room, or have a more demure personality, a meet-and-greet might not be the best option for your campaign. This will just highlight your shortcomings and provide fodder for your opponent. You can have the same results as large meet-and-greet by staging several smaller meetings in a more comfortable environment that shows you can relate to your potential constituents.

Assessing your staff's social skills

With so many people likely to attend your meet-and-greet, you do not want to have voters standing around thinking they are being ignored while others talk to you. This is where your staff and supporters come in. Your staff can talk with voters while you are busy with others.

Your staff should be courteous and listen to all points of view without being committal. The staff should understand they represent the candidate, and arguing with potential voters will reflect badly on the candidate. Voters will walk away from the meet-and-greet happier if they think the candidate has heard their voices. If they cannot talk to you directly, they want to know the message will get to you.

As you assessed your own strengths in a crowded room, you must do the same with your staff members. Not everyone can work with people spontaneously, so by gauging your staff's strengths and weaknesses, you can put the best people in appropriate places. Many jobs can be done at a meet-and-greet, including welcoming people, making sure all the guests sign in so you can mail campaign materials to them later, and managing the flow of people in and out of the event. By knowing your staff's strengths, you can make the event a boost for your campaign.

What are your strengths?

Not only do you need to assess the personal strengths of both you and your staff, but you also need to look at the strengths of your campaign. Which part of your message resonates the most with voters? If you plan to win votes with a family-first platform, consider including your family members in the meet-and-greet to emphasize that appearance. If business development is your strong suit, include local business leaders who support you at the meet-and-greet to talk about what you will do for your constituents. If crime prevention is your message, involve police officials or other city officials in your meet-and-greet to back you up.

Emphasize your message by showing voters you are already working to get these changes in place and you have made contacts within the community to start making things happen. Potential voters should see you involved in community issues and events. Keep the focus of any campaign event on your message. This will continually remind people why they should vote for you.

CASE STUDY: COUNCILWOMAN USES A WIDE VARIETY OF CAMPAIGN STRATEGIES

Barb Brady
Ward 4 Council member
Vermilion, Ohio

I have run for the Ward 4 council seat and won three consecutive times. I first decided to run to be proactive in representing the people of my neighborhood. At the time, there was a project being proposed for our subdivision, which many in the area felt was not in the residents' best interests. At that time, it appeared that getting involved with city council was the best way to be proactive.

During my campaign, I took advantage of every opportunity to interact with the public, which included a meet the candidates night at Vermilion High School. I had my résumé printed in the local newspapers and took advantage of a local cable spot. I also had yard signs made up and distributed throughout my ward. However, what I felt was the most beneficial form of campaigning was going door to door. I knocked on every door in my ward at least twice and left fliers during my campaign. I found the personal contact with voters to be crucial to my campaign and beneficial to my future position. It gave me the opportunity to talk to the other people in my ward about the things they wanted to see happen in our area and in Vermilion as a whole. The most challenging part about meeting with voters at their doors is to find time to do it other than during an election.

I chose not to do fundraising. I was able to keep the costs of my campaign within reason and paid for the endeavor myself. One of the ways I have been able to save money on campaigning is by recycling my yard signs. Because I did not have a year put on the sign when I ordered them, I was able to use the same signs in my second and third campaigns.

Throughout my campaign, I avoided any sort of negative campaigning. I believe voters have a hard enough time discerning fact from fiction during an election; they do not need candidates making it harder. Our jobs as candidates should be to inform and educate the voters about what we support and what we plan to do if elected.

The best advice I could give someone thinking about running for a political office is to think for themselves. It is easy to go along with the group, but it is not always what needs to be done. Nothing exciting happens when seven people sit around a table and always agree with each other. Ask the hard questions, grow a thick skin, and listen and be willing to change.

Working with Local Business Leaders

Few people have as vested an interest in local politics as local business leaders. The policies and laws local government bodies pass can directly impact their bottom line. Striking a balance between providing what businesses need to thrive and doing what is best for the city and the people is a line all candidates must walk.

Campaign contributions

Business leaders are the heart and soul of campaign fundraising. This means the biggest chance for the appearance of financial impropriety rests in the relationship between candidate and business leader.

Some business owners might wish to remain anonymous when contributing to a campaign out of fear of retribution if the other candidate wins. Although this might seem a bit paranoid, consider that local businesses are not huge conglomerations. Their service in a municipality is probably tenuous, and if they get on the wrong side of a future local leader, it could be detrimental to their company and their livelihood.

If a contributor wishes to remain unknown, tell him or her you will not advertise that he or she gave to your campaign, but if someone wants to check the campaign's books, it is not legal for you to not disclose where the money came from. Be gracious if he or she will not contribute at that point because you might have to work with him or her once you take office.

Explaining your platform

During a campaign, business leaders are interested in how you will keep the municipality's economy healthy and growing. This should be a main part of any platform when running for local office. A big part of local government is to help bring new businesses to the area to provide jobs and services to the people it governs. It is a competitive world for small governments when neighboring towns vie for businesses and the jobs they bring.

Therefore, having a strong economic plan is important to your message, but like anything else, many different schools of thought exist about economic development. You need to know your stance and be able to explain it clearly and definitively. Business leaders do not like to hear hesitation or doubt in the voices of their government officials. They want a strong leader who will take on any challenge that threatens the health and well-being of the company they have cultivated. Explain your plan to them whenever possible, and listen to the feedback you receive. During town hall meetings, meet-and-greets, and other public appearances, you need to be firm and sure with your vision but also show you are willing to listen to ideas.

Balancing community and commerce needs

What is good for business might not always look good for the average voter. Although a cut in taxes for small businesses might mean more commerce and a growing economy, it might also mean the tax burden is being placed on the regular taxpayer. It is important to create balance by offering incentives and benefits for both individuals and businesses. Keep the health of the community as a whole at the forefront of your campaign.

This balance is one every politician must keep, and it requires a good understanding of the economics of your electorate. Having a full understanding of the economic conditions in the area you plan to serve will enable you to tailor your goals and message to fit the needs of the community. Talk with local economic development boards and the chamber of commerce to find out which issues are facing businesses. Do not stop there; commerce is a two-way street. You need producers and consumers. Find out what the consumers are saying as well.

For example, the local business community might want to have a new hotel complex built to bring more visitors to the area, but the community as a whole might be against a surge in visitors. As a local leader, it will be your job to determine the right balance for issues like this. In this example, bringing more people to the town might not be the answer. It could work out fine, but it could also cause congestion in the area, which might hinder the town. Are the feelings of the community justified, or will the hotel complex be built in such a way the regular taxpayer will feel a minimal impact?

These are the types of issues you will have to deal with when balancing the community's needs against the needs of the businesses in your area. The best way to deal with these issues is to become well-informed. Do your homework, and talk with experts. When you are faced with answering questions about these issues in a public forum, you will be able to talk intelligently on the issue. The answer might not make everyone happy, but you will appear well versed and professional. Although they cannot all agree with your opinion on the matter, if they can agree you have done the needed work and research, they can still respect you and will be more likely to vote for you.

Reaching Out to Local Government Officials

The minute you decide to run for a government office, you become part of the government system regardless of whether you like it. The issues you raise in your campaign, the reflections you make, and the platform you run on become part of the public discussion on how the local government operates. Because of this, it is important to reach out to local leaders while campaigning. Not all positions are up for re-election at the same time, so these are the same people you would work with if you were elected into office. Your willingness to listen to them will be the foundation of a good working relationship once you are elected.

Talking to current government officials can also give you a better understanding of why certain decisions were made. Sometimes, a government body simply cannot bend to the wishes of the population regardless of how much the public wants something due to rules and regulations. Investigating the whole story can keep you from making campaign promises you cannot keep, which you will be judged on later when you run for re-election.

Local government officials can also help your campaign. These are people who found a way to get elected during their election and might have the voters on their side. When going to other officials for guidance and support, it is important to be humble. No one likes to be told how to do their job, and seasoned politicians are no exception. Although you do not need to follow every bit of advice you receive, be gracious for the advice and respect their experience.

Endorsements from emergency personnel

The most visible arm of any local government is its emergency services. Fire trucks, police cars, and ambulances are vehicles few people can miss, and for the most part, emergency crews are well-respected in communities for providing their services. Working with these groups throughout your campaign and receiving an endorsement from these groups can be an invaluable boost to your election effort.

The No. 1 thing people want from their government is a feeling of safety. If you have the backing of the police and fire departments because you have worked with them to determine their needs, the voters will see their safety is a top concern. In addition, the high visibility of these individuals increases the likelihood your campaign can become associated with the men and women who keep your constituents safe.

Working with the bureaucracy

Not all administrative officials are elected, and many of these bureaucrats will continue to work for the new government after the election is over. How well you work with them will determine how much help you can get during your campaign and beyond.

You will be in frequent contact with the clerk before and during your campaign because you will need to work with the clerk's office to submit your nomination forms. Although the official clerk is elected in local government, the clerk's office is staffed with professionals who might have worked for several different clerks and government bodies. That is true for many other areas of government in which consistency is key to helping the government run smoothly.

These bureaucrats are your best resource for finding out what the needs of the local government are. By raising some of these issues during your campaign, you can show voters you are in tune with the needs of government workers.

As with emergency personnel, build these relationships to receive endorsements. This will show voters you are ready to work with those who are currently employed with the government, which can hint those who know the most about local government think you are the best person for the job.

Receiving endorsements from elected officials

Besides endorsements from officials in the department for which you are seeking election, endorsements from elected officials in other municipalities and government offices can also be a big boost. You see examples of this at the national level when a president or senator endorses a candidate for governor or another national office. Although it is unlikely you will get the president to endorse you in a local election, you could meet with officials of another city and ask them for their endorsement. Additionally, if the politician who previously held the seat you are running for is not your opponent, you can approach that person for an endorsement. As long as he or she was popular with the voters, that endorsement can be beneficial. When asking for an endorsement, explain your platform and how you will work with surrounding communities to make the area a better place to live.

Aside from showing you are "in the know" and have been in contact with government officials, seeking endorsements from other elected officials will also raise the level of trust others have in you. When voters hear of another elected official backing a candidate, it might pique their interest in what you have to say. Of course, the biggest pitfall of this technique is making sure the candidates who back you are trustworthy themselves and popular with your constituents. You do not want to associate yourself with unpopular politicians because that will make you look untrustworthy in the eyes of the voters. Also, make sure no current conflicts are simmering between your electorate and that politician's area.

For example, if an industry is looking to build a new factory in your town or another nearby town, an endorsement from the mayor of the other town might not be in your best interest. To voters, it might seem as though you are in their corner and do not have your constituents' interests at heart. When receiving endorsements, think of the ramifications of each endorsement and the way that endorsement coincides with your message. You do not want to have your message say one thing while the people who endorse you are sending out a different message.

Political Parties

Depending on the type of election you are in, you might have to work with political party personnel, such as campaign managers or volunteers. Working with a political party can help those new to local government because they get to use the party's expertise in all areas of campaigning. In addition, they can receive support from some voters simply for belonging to a certain party because some voters simply choose to vote the party line. However, working with political parties also has its drawbacks because you might compromise some of what you set out to do in exchange for the party's support.

Political parties have been around since the beginning of our government. America primarily functions under a two-party system with the occasional third-party candidate or independent gaining an election victory. As a candidate, you can choose to join a political party or run as an independent. Although the choice is up to you, political parties supply support through volunteers, campaign funds, and campaign professionals who can make a difference in a close race.

Advantages and disadvantages

The advantages of working with a political party are the support, funds, and expertise you receive. If you are running for a seat that requires you to run under a party affiliation, chances are the party apparatus in your area operates like a well-oiled machine. The volunteers and campaign experts who will assist you have been through all this before. They know where the votes are and from which areas you need to win voters. All this will help you save time and money when crafting your message.

The disadvantage of working with a political party is that you are now associated with that party and what that party does. This affiliation is not limited to what the party is doing in your local area. You will be affiliated with what that party is doing at the state and national levels. In many cases, the party has already chosen its platform and the sides it will take on many issues. Local political parties, of course, know the local issues, and there is flexibility in the local party to take a different side if necessary to win the election. The bottom line, however, is you can't make all decisions on where you stand on an issue.

When do you need a political party?

Weighing the advantages or disadvantages of working with a political party might be a moot point if you live in an area or are running for an office that requires you to choose a party. In some parts of the country, the choice is obvious. Other times, the office might serve too many constituents not to be part of a political party. The mayor of New York City, for example, likely needs the backing of a political apparatus to successfully win in a city with nearly 4 million voters. An independent candidate might not have the resources or the expertise to reach a large number of voters to win that election. Even offices that serve fewer constituents sometimes need to be tied to political parties. Many county positions require you to be part of a political party to have a real chance at winning because the political parties have a lot of influence.

Nonparty positions

Small communities might not require you to be part of a political party to be voted into office. School boards are a good example of this. Most school boards simply replace members by taking the number of candidates with the most votes according to the number of seats open. In races such as these, political parties are not as influential because the electorate is small enough for a single candidate to get their message to the voters by themselves. There is also not much in it for the political party. A political party is not likely to spend time and money on an election that only impacts a small geographic or demographic area.

It might also be detrimental to the candidate's efforts to be involved with a political party. In some positions, it is more important to voters their elected official is responsive to them than be a member of a political party. A member of a school board, for example, who is connected with a political party might be viewed as having the interests of the party at heart rather than the interests of the children who attend that area's schools.

Sometimes not being affiliated with a political party can work to your advantage. Affiliations with a political party might make voters feel the candidate will work more for the party than the local area. However, not being affiliated with a party will keep voters focused on what you plan to do for their community. The same can be said for smaller municipalities, such as towns and villages, where the voters have easy access to their elected officials.

In each of these cases, the need for the local population to have independent representatives and the lack of incentive for political parties to move into those areas lessens a candidate's need for party support.

Reaching out From the Comfort of Your Home

In addition to all the traditional forms of campaigning, which have been discussed in this chapter, political campaigns have gone online in recent years. Candidates are making use of online communities, social networking websites, personal websites, and blogs to carry the message to the voters. *Chapter 7 is dedicated to using this technology and understanding its role in political campaigning.* The following checklist, however, will help lead you through the campaigning process.

☑ CHAPTER CHECKLIST

- ❑ Choose campaigning methods.
- ❑ Buy advertising space in newspapers and time on the radio and television.
- ❑ Organize town hall meetings or local debates with your opponent.
- ❑ Organize and attend several meet-and-greets.
- ❑ Distribute yard signs to supporters.
- ❑ Approach local businesses to gain support.
- ❑ Seek out valuable endorsements.

CHAPTER 7

Technology and Campaigning

Twenty years ago, candidates had few options for contacting potential voters. Phone calls; newspaper, radio and television ads; and direct mailing were some of the only options. Today, with the emergence of the Internet and cell phone technologies, candidates can instantly contact supporters and spread their message to more people. Using the Internet and social networking websites throughout the course of a campaign is almost expected at this point. As mentioned in Chapter 6, newspaper readership is considerably down. That is not because people stopped caring about the news; people are getting their information from other sources, especially the Internet.

The other aspect of the technological revolution in campaigning is these methods cost little to nothing. A website, blog, or social media site can be set up for a fraction of the cost of a television, radio, or newspaper ad, and in many cases, these means of advertising are absolutely free. Although they could be expensive if you chose to bring in design and technology professionals, you can limit those costs by finding a tech-savvy volunteer to organize your online campaign efforts. Many forms of social media are so simple the candidate can make updates from his or her phone while on the road.

Social Media

The most recent advancement in campaigning is social networking, which is helping candidates reach a larger audience. Facebook, Twitter, LinkedIn, and other websites can help you spread your message to supporters and followers without costing you anything. Although the exact definition is still evolving, social networking generally refers to using an online community that enables people to connect and communicate with others. Although the format varies from one network to another, communication takes place through multiple means and channels, such as blogs, e-mail, instant messaging, forums, video, and chat rooms.

Using a social networking site is cheap, and it shows you are a technically savvy candidate who keeps up with new advancements. Even if a voter is not on Facebook or Twitter, he or she likely knows those sites are popular, and you can win points for simply showing you use them. In addition, social networking opens your campaign to younger voters, which are an emerging force in elections. College groups, such as the Young Republicans and Young Democrats, are active groups that vote in the cities and counties in which they live. Although you might not align yourself with a political party, these politically active youths might use your Facebook or Twitter page to find out more about you. This could lead to votes and volunteers.

You can also use these sites to seek out possible voters. These sites have search features that allow you to look for people based on where they are, what they are saying on the Internet, or who they are friends with. You can send messages to these possible voters and ask them to join your network and spread the word about your candidacy.

How it will help

Members of social networking sites are numerous, which creates an excellent opportunity for an individual to expand and promote themselves without having to pay for advertising. With social networking, you can build your name recognition and your image and grow your base of supporters. In addition to giving potential voters another way to become familiar with you as a candidate, social networking sites will also lead people to your website. Your website is where you will keep all the information about yourself as a candidate and your campaign. Your website can include links to news articles that are relevant to the campaign. Your website will also include announcements for fundraising events, rallies, and campaign appearances. Your website can also be a means of volunteering or donating money. The following are some ideas on how to use social networking websites to increase traffic to your website:

- Link from your website to your social network profile. Creating a link will allow visitors of your social networking site to go directly from there to your website.

- Use social bookmarking to increase your website's exposure on social networking sites. Bookmarking your website on social networking sites will increase your visibility and make it easier for visitors to find your website.

- Create and share videos and photos on Flickr and YouTube that describe your background, qualifications, platform, and message. Providing pictures and videos of yourself for potential voters to view online will make you more recognizable in the community.

- Use social networking forums to promote yourself, your website, and your blog.

Social networking websites

The following social networking sites can prove beneficial to your campaign.

Facebook®

Facebook (**www.facebook.com**) is the leading social networking site. Initially, Facebook was developed to connect university students. Eventually, the site became available publicly and expanded to users of all ages, and its popularity exploded. Businesses, organizations, and charities use Facebook as a marketing tool, and it can be useful to politicians and political candidates as well. There are about 600 million active Facebook users. Facebook makes it easy to add friends, send messages, and create communities or event invitations. Candidates can easily set up a personal page and invite supporters to become friends or set up a fan page through which supporters can become fans of the candidate. Either way, the candidate will be able to leave brief messages for their supporters and important reminders for up-coming debates and election day. Supporters will also have the opportunity to respond to the candidate and offer their support and encouragement. The candidate can also link his or her Face-book page to his or her website so friends or fans can easily ac-cess the campaign website.

MySpace®

MySpace (**www.myspace.com**) is a social networking web-site that offers an interactive platform for all its users. It allows the sharing of files, pictures, and even music videos. Users of-ten compare Facebook to MySpace, but MySpace allows more personalization when designing pages. Candidates can set up a MySpace page that is personalized to reflect their values, ideas, and campaign message. Use of the two sites would be the same for an electoral race. Candidates can set up a page to update their supporters on information about the race and link support-ers back to the candidate's website.

YouTube®

YouTube (**www.youtube.com**) is another social networking site Google owns. YouTube is the most popular video sharing net-work site, and it is a place to do video marketing. Candidates can use YouTube to share video messages with others and share vid-eo coverage of fundraising events, speeches, rallies, and debates. YouTube videos can be shared through MySpace and Facebook and can be embedded on the candidate's website. Ron Paul is an example of a candidate who used YouTube to spread his mes-sage. Viewers could access and view multiple Ron Paul speeches during his campaign.

Twitter™

The popularity of Twitter (**http://twitter.com**) has grown at an amazing rate likely because it is different from other social networking sites. Twitter is a form of microblogging, which is a Web service that allows users to broadcast short messages — in Twitter's case 140 characters or fewer — to other users. With Twitter, you can let others know what you are doing throughout the day right from your phone or computer. When you sign up with Twitter, you can post and receive messages known as tweets™, and the site sends your tweet out to your followers. Twitter will allow supporters to follow you on the campaign trail. You can add brief updates throughout the day to let people know where you are or where you are heading.

Twitter is a way to stay in contact with Internet users, but it should not be the only social networking website candidates use. Although the number of Internet users with a registered Twitter account is growing by the millions each year, Twitter's retention rate is only 40 percent when compared to Facebook and MySpace, which have retention rates of 70 percent. One of the useful aspects of Twitter is you can have your Twitter account updated without doing anything. When you set up a Twitter account, you will be given the option to link the Twitter account to a Facebook account. If you chose this option, anything posted on Facebook will automatically update Twitter. Although other social networking websites might be more beneficial, Twitter is one more way to reach potential voters.

Flickr®

Flickr (**www.flickr.com**) is a photo and video sharing website that lets you organize and store your photos online. You can upload photos from your desktop, send them by e-mail, or upload photos taken on your camera phone. It has features to eliminate red eye, crop a photo, or use your creative side to add fonts and effects. Flickr will allow you to publish your campaign photos online, and these can be linked to from your website. Google Picasa® (**http://picasa.google.com**) is another photo sharing and storing application.

E-mail

E-mail can be used to keep supporters, volunteers, and voters updated on campaign activity. When the opportunity arises, you should collect e-mail addresses from potential voters. Create a regularly updated e-mail list so every possible person is receiving your e-mail. Because you can only e-mail those who have supplied you with their e-mail addresses, e-mail can be used as a means of staying in contact with supporters. E-mail should provide event information and address people individually to either thank them for their support or to invite them to an event.

The positive aspect of using e-mail to connect with others is you can send information to a select group of people or send out a single private message. Social networking websites, such as Facebook, are public, and depending on your privacy settings, anyone can read what you write. This includes your opposition.

The downside to e-mail is you need to be able to collect a supporters' e-mail address to contact him or her, and you have no guarantee he or she will read your e-mail. Most people are bombarded with junk e-mail every day, so they skim through their inboxes and only read messages that look important.

Website

A website has also become a necessary tool in campaigning. People expect to be able to find information instantly on the Internet, including information about candidates in local elections. In an upcoming election, voters will expect to be able to visit your website and have answered their questions about your message or your plan if elected. Candidates are able to completely control the message on their website and know that people will visit the website to find out information only about him or her. Personal websites can be linked to any of the social networking websites discussed in the previous section and personal blogs, which will be discussed in the next section.

Websites cost money to create, but a good website can still often be built for less than what a newspaper, radio, or television ad costs. Furthermore, a website can be more inclusive of your message, contain any information you would like it to, and change according to how the needs of your campaign change. Having a good website that is easy to navigate and looks good is a must and will make your campaign look more professional. If you do not have Web design skills and do not know someone who does, it would be a good idea to hire an outside person or company to design the site for you. Your website will be the face of your campaign.

Your website should include a wide variety of information on your message, your goals as a candidate, and information on current issues in the community. You should keep an updated calendar of events on your website and a countdown to election day. You can include links to your social networking pages. Your website should also include a way for voters to contact you with questions, suggestions, or gestures of support. Additionally, your website should be set up to accept credit card or PayPal payments from those who wish to donate to your campaign.

CHOOSING A WEB DESIGNER

Hiring a professional to design your website can be costly, so shop around to find the service you want for a price you can afford. Web design companies cost as few as a couple thousand for a complete website or as much as $50,000. When choosing a professional, meet with the designer personally to determine whether he or she understands the image you are trying to create. Also understand exactly what will be included in the cost. You will need to decide whether you just need the site designed or need someone to continually update and build your website.

Although you should get services donated when possible to reduce costs, you also want to make sure the website accurately represents you and your message. If a volunteer comes forward and offers to create your website, sit down with him or her first to see the type of work he or she has done in the past. You might decide to hire a professional to do the original design and use a volunteer to keep the website updated.

Blogs

Another way to reach potential voters is through a blog. In their simplest form, blogs are like Web-based diaries that allow you to publish your thoughts on any subject. Blogs are a way to reach possible voters and make connections with them. Blog posts are written with specific keywords in mind. For example, if the local school system is a major discussion during the campaign, you can purposely use the words Elyria School Board in an article you are writing about the election. When someone in your area searches for information about Elyria schools, your blog post might appear as an option. Blog posts can also address specific issues and concerns. A blog post can be a cross between a researched article and a personal reflection. Blogs should be written using casual language and can cover any topic you wish. It is best to stay away from the bland newspaper style of writing when crafting your blog.

Rather, you should make your blog personal. Talk about something interesting that happened while you were campaigning that day, and use names of people you met. By keeping the writing anecdotal, people will feel as though you are letting them into your private world, which can increase the level of trust they feel for you. You must be careful, though, when writing a blog. The informal style can sometimes lead people to get too personal. You want to make sure you never say anything that could offend or turn off voters to your message.

When writing blog posts, you want to provide links to your other blog posts and articles on your website. When a reader finds one of your blog posts and becomes interested, providing these links will make it easy for the reader to find other information about you and your message. Linking your blog posts to your social networking website will also allow your social networking friends and followers to read all your blog posts. Writing blog posts, maintaining a website, and using social networking pages might seem like a lot of extra work, but the purpose of all this is to be readily accessible to potential voters and increase voter recognition.

POSSIBLE BLOG TOPICS

The following are examples of topics you can discuss in your blog:

- Specific campaign goals fully explained

- An explanation of your work history and educational background

- The way the economy has affected your area

- Ways in which you plan to attract new businesses and jobs to the area

- Your history with the area (include whether you grew up in the same town)

- What you love most about the area in which you live

- Specific reasons you feel you are the best candidate for the position

- What you feel are the greatest needs in your area

- What you plan to do to address those needs

The construction of a blog

Although a multitude of different programs are available for starting a blog, each program offers the same basic construction, which is the following:

- **Title:** The title of the blog provides the blog reader with an idea of what the blog as a whole is about. If you only plan to maintain the blog for the election, the title can be as simple as your name and campaign slogan. If you plan to maintain the blog throughout your term of office, you can choose a title that will represent you and the area.

- **Date:** Blogs are displayed in reverse chronological order, so the most recent post and the date posted are at the top.

- **Post title:** Each blog post has a title.

- **Blog text:** The actual text of each blog post follows the title.

- **Blog post information:** This includes the individual who or business that wrote the blog and sometimes contact information.

- **Blogger comments:** The blog will have an area for readers to leave comments, responses, opinions, or reactions to a blog post. This is not a mandatory field; if your intent is only to push information out via your blog, you do not have to accept comments. However, if you do accept comments, you should have them monitored. When you set up the blog, you will have the option to limit the comments to approved comments only. When you do this, every comment will only be made readable on your blog after you have approved it. This will allow you to filter out negative comments or spam.

- **Previous blog posts:** After the most recent blog post will be a reverse chronological listing of previous blog posts.

- **Archived posts:** The blog keeps a history of old posts, which are not visible, but can still be accessed. Even the best blogs get unwieldy; it is not uncommon to archive old posts after a preset period of time.

- **Blogroll:** The blogroll links to other related sites. This might include the websites or blogs of other candidates you support and your local political party website.

- **Advertising:** This is a common sight in the world of blogging. Many advertisements are prominently featured in free blogging applications. In some cases, you can generate revenue through the use of advertising, but often, these are third-party advertisements you must tolerate to use the blogging software.

- **Feeds:** These allow people to subscribe to your blog. When they do this, the feed will automatically send them your new blog posts as you publish them. This will prevent your readers from missing a blog post.

TIPS AND INFORMATION TO KEEP IN MIND WHILE BLOGGING

The more traffic you attract to your blog, the more traffic you can send to your website. Blogging is more than just writing about something you find interesting and relevant. You need to keep your audience and your goals in mind when writing a blog post. The following advice will help you make sure you are doing the things you need to get the greatest number of people to see your blog:

- **Your blog is public.** It is on the Internet for anyone to read. Although you might only be targeting a specific audience, everyone can read it and post comments. Make sure it is appropriate and sends the message you intend.

- **A blog is not for you.** It is for your constituents. Write for the reader. Tailor your blog posts to the concerns of the community. Consider what your voters want to read about rather than what you want to write about.

- **Expect SPAM comments.** Likewise, expect negative, argumentative, and insulting comments. You can remove these comments, which is time consuming, or you can roll with the punches. Kill them with kindness, stay relevant, stick to your ground rules, and push your message. You will not make everyone happy all the time, so do not try.

- **Expect positive comments on your blog.** When you get them, take the time to thank the individual.

- **Update your blog on a regular basis.** If you update daily, you should stick to that routine. If you cannot commit to that, do it weekly. Your readers will expect updates on a periodic basis.

- **Include RSS or Atom feeds on your blog.** This allows people to subscribe and receive your blog updates automatically.

- **Make sure your links are clearly defined.** Include a description of the links that are included in your blog to indicate where the links lead.

- **Always respond to comments.** Your readers post comments for a reason: They expect a response. Blogs are designed to be sources of two-way communication.

- **Correct typos and errors in your blogs.** Your blog writing reflects your ability to communicate effectively to those who read it. Have your communications staff edit posts before they are published.

- **Do not write anything you do not want anyone else to know about.** If you write it, it might come back to haunt you later. Do not write anything you do not want the whole word to know.

Closing out the campaign

Developing an online presence is an important part of a successful campaign. Reducing costs by using the free resources already available will not reduce exposure. The following checklist will help you on your way.

☑ CHAPTER CHECKLIST

☐ Choose the social networking websites you are most comfortable using.

☐ Set up a campaign website with your information, experience, and message along with photos and a calendar of events.

☐ Look into a Web design company if necessary.

☐ Create a blog and link it to your website for online visitors to easily access.

☐ Create links from your website to your social networking pages.

☐ Update regularly. It does not need to be daily, but your supporters want to hear from you.

CHAPTER 8

Know Your Opponent

I n any contest, whether it is a sporting event, business take-over, or war, if you do not know your opponents strengths or weaknesses, you have little chance of coming out victorious. The same is true in politics. Knowing your opponent is key to success. Finding out information about your opponent is something you will need to start as soon as you decide to run for office, and you will continue to do this until the votes are in and the election is over. Your opponent's strengths and weaknesses should be included in your campaign plan.

In small local elections, you might know your opponent even before you have decided to run for public office. In other cases, he or she might be a complete stranger, and you might have no idea what he or she stands for. Research your opponent's platform as soon as possible, and determine how it relates to your platform and the issues people are talking about.

Finding out your opponent's stance on certain issues does not entail an espionage mission to infiltrate his or her headquarters; however, it might mean reading his or her campaign materials, talking to supporters to find out what they are saying on the streets, or simply listening to what the public is saying about your opponent. The bottom line: You need to know what your opponent is going to do and what his or her message is so you can be prepared to answer any questions that come your way.

What You Do Not Know Can Hurt You

Know your opponent's campaign and platform so you can explain to voters how you are different. If two candidates seem the same, a voter is less likely to feel motivated to pick either one. You do not want to be on the campaign trail touting the same message as your opponent. Also, you want to be able to address the differences in your campaign in an intelligent manner. If you know the differences ahead of time, you can present a well-thought argument.

If you are running against the incumbent or a politician who is experienced in a different position, have a detailed account of all their actions while in office. *Table 4 on page 197 provides locations at which this information can be located.* This will allow you to have a good picture of your opponent's successes and downfalls. You will also be able to use this information when referencing the differences between your message and the message your opponent has been delivering while in office.

Your opponent's strengths and weaknesses

There is no doubt pointing out character flaws in an opposing political candidate has worked in the past, but that is not what this section is talking about. In this case, you simply want to know the strengths and weaknesses in your opponent's message. For example, if your opponent's message focuses on bettering the local school system, and his or her voting history supports this agenda, the opponent has a strong message. However, if your opponent expresses working hard for the community, but his or her voting history shows they missed several votes, you can easily argue the opponent is not working hard for the community. This would be a clear weakness in his or her message. Not everyone is going to be happy with all aspects of a candidate's message. And in some cases, those aspects can help your campaign, especially if your platform already addresses that issue.

Pointing out these difference in a friendly way can help you stand out from your opponent. By simply pointing out your opponent has stated he or she stands on one side of an issue, you can emphasize you stand on the other side. This can show voters they have a choice between the vision your opponent offers and yours.

Also, if you learn your opponent's strengths, you can avoid running into situations in which your opponent has an edge. For instance, if your opponent is an excellent public speaker, challenging him or her to a debate might not be a good idea. On the other hand, if your opponent is not a good public speaker, trying to draw him or her into a public forum might be a good strategy.

Your opponent's support

Understanding where your opponent's support is coming from is another key element in getting to know your opponent. Learning who will be voting for your opponent in an upcoming election can help you tailor your message. Look at your opponent's message and determine why it appeals to the supporters he or she has amassed. In which ways do the opponent's supporters differ from those who support you? The answer to this question will tell you whether it is worth going after voters who are currently in your opponent's camp. For example, unions are a major issue in many local areas. If your opponent has a strong history of supporting unions, union members are likely to continue supporting your opponent regardless of how strong your campaign is. In this situation, it might be best to focus your energy and resources on voters who do not have a dedicated history with a specific candidate.

This can also allow you to tailor your campaign strategy to attract some of those voters. For example, if an issue your opponent is touting could fit into your message, it might benefit you to agree with your opponent and show you are on the same side. To use the example of union members again, just because you believe unions will support your opponent in the upcoming election does not mean you should not make it public if you are in favor of unions. Some of those voters might have been unhappy with your opponent in other areas and would be willing to support you because you are pro-union. You must be careful when doing this because you do not want to alienate your current supporters, but persuading voters to switch sides and support you over your opponent can be the knockout blow in an election.

The following table shows a list of considerations for conducting research into your opponent. Not all the information in the following table will be attainable because it might not be made available to the public, but you should get as much information as you can. Examine everything you collect to extract important information you can use during the campaign. This information should be kept with the campaign plan under opponent's strengths and weaknesses.

Table 4: Opponent Research

INFORMATION NEEDED	WHERE TO FIND IT	WHAT TO LOOK FOR
Public voting history	County board of elections	When the candidate registered, history of changing parties, consistency
Employment record	Human resources department at current or past employer	Work history, performance reports, safety violations, infractions
Campaign finance reports	County board of elections, elections clerk, or secretary of state	How much the candidate is able to raise, undesirable expenses, family on payroll
Official voting record	Clerk of board where the candidate served	Legislation or projects the candidate proposed or supported
Official meeting minutes	Clerk of board where the candidate served	Attendance, conflicts, silly statements
Video of official meetings	Clerk of board where candidate served	Physical evidence of statements, conflicts, attendance, controversial votes
Newspaper clippings	Library microfilm archives or the Internet	Any headlines involving the candidate
Ethics disclosure reports	State ethics commission, secretary of state	Improper reporting, inconsistency

INFORMATION NEEDED	WHERE TO FIND IT	WHAT TO LOOK FOR
Criminal history	County clerk of courts, municipal clerk, local police department	Any criminal history, including a large amount of unpaid tickets
Property records	County auditor, assessor, recorder, or clerk	Properties the candidate owns
Civil history	County or municipal clerk	Liens of judgments against candidate

Facing your opponent

Voters like to see two candidates in the same room answering the same questions because it makes it easier to compare the two and determine who the better candidate is. In a tight race, you inevitably will be asked to face your opponent in some manner. This is often in the form of debates. Although they can be intimidating, debates are an important part of campaigning and should not be avoided.

Facing your opponent will provide you with valuable opportunities to use the research you collected about your opponent. If you find information that is inconsistent with his or her campaign message, you can question him or her about the inconsistency and force your opponent to explain him or herself to the voters rather than giving your opponent the opportunity to focus on his or her message. However, be aware that your opponent will have done equally extensive research on you and might not hesitate to make the information they find public. There is a fine line between challenging an opponent and negatively campaigning. *Negative campaigning will be discussed in the next chapter.* It is important to keep debates and discussions about issues relevant to the election rather than making the conflict personal.

Debates

Debates are the most common way political candidates face each other. Debates are structured events at which a moderator asks each candidate a question. For a debate, know the strengths and weaknesses of your opponent and your own. For example, avoid the topic if you are not fully comfortable discussing your educational background, but be prepared with a response if your opponent brings it up. It is better to know your opponent's pluses and minuses when you debate because you can use them against him or her. For example, if you know from your research questioning your opponent about his or her voting history causes this opponent to get flustered, revisit the topic as often as possible. Likewise, if your opponent is well versed in the local school system and the problems it faces, it would be best not to directly challenge him or her on the topic unless you feel confident you can sound as sure as your opponent.

If your opponent is taking a stance on an issue that is not as popular as your stance, you can use the debate to highlight the way the two of you are different. You can show voters you are listening to their needs by making references to people you have talked to or experiences you have had. Know your weaknesses so you can prepare before the debate to defend them because you know your opponent is likely to raise these issues during the debate. Then, you can explain why you have a certain stance on an issue or did something in the past. This can make you seem confident and in control of your message — two things voters are looking for in a candidate.

Classical debates are styled after school debates. Each candidate will stand at a podium facing a moderator who will ask specific questions. Once a question is asked, each candidate will have an opportunity to answer the question and rebut what the other candidate said. Debate responses are timed, and once a candidate's time is up, it is up to the moderator to move on to the next question. Another type of debate is an open forum, or town hall debate, which is discussed in the next section.

Open forums

Open forums, like town hall meetings and public gatherings, are a way to show how you stand out from your opponent in a more social and personal setting. In an open forum debate, the candidates are each given the opportunity to answer questions potential voters who attend the event ask. The questions are not pre-screened, and the candidates will not know them before the moderator asks. This forces candidates to answer questions they might not have prepared for. This type of environment forces candidates to think quickly while remaining calm and professional. If being in this type of environment is one of your opponent's weaknesses, you can win points with the voters as long as it is one of your strengths.

This is also a way to test whether your message is easy to understand compared to your opponent's. If your opponent needs to explain aspects of his or her message to individuals but voters can quickly understand your message, your message might be more generally appealing to the public. Of course, the opposite is also true. If you spend a lot of time explaining your message but your opponent is having an easy time of it, you might need to tweak your approach.

Public appearances

There are multiple opportunities for you and your opponent to meet voters at the same public events. Parades, fairs, and picnics are ways to get in touch with voters and show you are a candidate people can trust. You can gain voters' trust by being approachable and open to discussion and questions during public appearances. Making frequent public appearances is essential during a campaign, and you should not avoid them out of fear of confrontation. Frequent public appearances will make it easier for people to connect your name with who you are rather than just seeing a name on yard signs.

When you run into your opponent in these noncontentious settings, you will not be pressed by questions or forced to debate with one another, and you should always be civil and gracious. This shows you are receptive to the ideas of others, are a good person to trust, and know how to work with people even when their views are different from your own. Sometimes, individuals who support your opponent ask challenging questions in public settings, which might make you feel forced to answer them or to debate with your opposition. Remain calm and avoid forced debates or verbal confrontations. Your opponent might also work to keep interactions calm and civil, but be prepared if your opponent tries to challenge you directly or go along with a supporter who is challenging you. This will go a long way with voters who are on the fence and agree with you on some issues and your opponent on other issues.

Strengths and weaknesses of your opponent's campaign

Now you have looked at the strengths and weaknesses of your opponent and the message he or she is relaying, you can also look at the way your opponent's campaign is structured and where the strengths and weaknesses are in it. Knowing how your opponent is running his or her campaign and spending or not spending money might help you determine where to spend your resources. For example, if your opponent is spending time speaking at local church events, you might want to consider the same. However, if your opponent is spending a large sum of money on television commercials, and you cannot afford to, consider increasing your door-to-door campaign to reach more voters. Always stick with the goals you set early on in the campaign, and do not merely react to what your opponent is doing. That said, you should look at the strategies your opponent is using to help you supplement your own strategies. If you see your opponent has been unsuccessful with direct mailings, learn from his or her mistakes and pursue a different means of getting your name and message to the voters. Although having a campaign plan is important, being flexible and willing to change your plan if you realize it is not working out the way you wanted is equally important.

Research how much money your opponent's campaign is spending and where that money is being spent. Which types of fundraisers is your opponent employing? If your opponent is holding fundraisers that cater to wealthy voters, it could be an opportunity for you to show the rest of the voters you care more about them than your opponent.

Also, find out which businesses are supporting your opponent. Businesses are a source of campaign contributions, so having their support is a boost to your coffers. Determining which businesses are siding with your opponent can help you decide whether you want to try to lure those companies away from your opponent or gain endorsements from competing businesses, even those in a completely different type of industry.

You should also find out about the type of endorsements your opponent is generating. Who is publicly backing your opponent, and why? Endorsements say a lot about your campaign and can be a boost or detriment to your campaign depending on the situation. *Endorsements are discussed in Chapter 6.* If your opponent is receiving endorsements from outside the municipality, you could use that to run a locally minded campaign that accentuates your opponent's efforts elsewhere. This will send the message to your voters that you are more focused on local groups and interests than your opponent is.

Getting dirty

Getting to know your opponent can ultimately lead you to an important and difficult choice: whether to point out character flaws, indiscretions, or other negative aspects of your opponent. Especially in local elections, in which candidates often know each other personally, several people in the area might know your opponent's faults or possible indiscretions. You might also be presented with unverifiable information about your opponent at some point during the campaign. You need to go over the information and the source of the information and then decide whether making the information public is the right thing to do and whether it will help or hurt your campaign. The decision to use this information to boost your campaign will fall on you, and what you decide could determine whether you win or lose the election. *Chapter 9 will help you decide whether to run a negative campaign.* The following checklist will help you research your opponent.

☑ CHAPTER CHECKLIST

- ☐ Conduct research into your opponent.
- ☐ Organize the information into a format you can easily read and examine.
- ☐ Make an extensive list of your opponent's strengths and weaknesses.
- ☐ Include all pertinent information about your opponent in your campaign plan.
- ☐ Consider which information can be used to boost your campaign and which should be held back.
- ☐ If some of the information is questionable, do more research to verify the information is correct.

CHAPTER 9

The Dark Side of Running for Political Office

A ttack ads, character assassinations, and backhanded tactics have become a familiar staple of the national and state campaign scene. Candidates running for president, a member of Congress, and governor spend millions producing ads that degrade their opponent or otherwise point out his or her failings and missteps. These tactics work in those realms because candidates for those offices consistently rely on negative campaigning as a way to get elected. But do these tactics carry over to local elections, and what should you consider as a candidate when deciding whether to employ these tactics? The goal of this chapter is to explore all sides of this often tricky issue so you can make an informed decision about the use of negative campaigning.

Slinging Mud

The term slinging mud describes the tactics that point out the negative aspects of your opponent's character or political past by attacking him or her professionally and personally. Slinging mud often involves using half-truths and suggestions of inappropriate behavior. You must choose whether you will get dirty and participate in a negative campaign as the campaign wears on. The decision you make should be based on a couple of key points that will help define your campaign and you as a candidate. By basing your decision on these factors, you can make the best decision for the situation.

Moral choice

The decision to enter into negative campaigning is first a moral choice. When running in a local election, the need for negative campaigning is small because you have many opportunities to get your message out to the voters in a positive manner. However, a time might come when it looks as though you will lose the election or when your opponent begins using shady tactics to harm your campaign. At this point, turning to a negative campaign might look like a good option.

One factor that should influence your decision is the nature of the information you have. If the negative information directly relates to the candidate's ability to perform the job or the candidate's past job performance, it applies to the election. Negative information about the candidate's past, family, or rumored indiscretions is not relevant to the campaign.

Even at the local level, the chance a negative campaign will produce results is good, especially when it counteracts a negative campaign from an opponent. However, partaking in a negative campaign can also turn voters against you. During an intense campaign, voters often grow tired of hearing and watching attack ads. By staying away from negative tactics, you can show you are above stooping to your opponent's level. Because the voting population is smaller than on the state and national level, you can easily defend yourself to the public. Show how you can affect the community in a positive way while portraying your opponent as a purely divisive force, which his or her use of negative campaign tactics exemplifies.

Does using these tactics fit the office you are running for?

If you feel running a negative campaign is necessary in your situation, another question you need to ask yourself is whether the office you are running for will support a candidate who uses such maneuvers. Will running a negative campaign make you appear tough and ready to take on the world, or will it make you look like a bully? Worse yet, will it look as though you are attacking your opponent to distract people from realizing you are not qualified?

The president, congressional representatives, and governors all must be tough, hard-nosed individuals who are ready to take on opponents and fight the opposing political party. Therefore, constituents can justify the candidate's use of negative campaigning as a weapon. However, appearing as a hard-nosed fighter might not best serve someone who is running for a local mayoral office or a city council seat.

If you have just come off a hard-fought, dirty campaign that left lasting hard feelings, you might not get the support you need to reach your goals when in office or be re-elected when your term is up. Local voters will want someone trustworthy who will work with others to better the city. They want someone they can approach and discuss problems with who won't use those problems as a weapon in an upcoming election.

Determining the office's ability to support such negative tactics is vital to choosing whether you will participate in negative campaigning. Your appearance as a trustworthy individual is key, and this is true at any level, which is why state and national candidates have developed ways to run negative ads while distancing themselves from the ads.

CASE STUDY: RUNNING A POSITIVE CAMPAIGN DESPITE OPPONENT ATTACKS

Eileen Bulan
Mayor
City of Vermilion

For 14 years, I worked for the City of Vermilion as the clerk of council. I then worked as the mayor's assistant for one year before spending 10 years in the position of director of public service. I had dedicated 25 years to the City of Vermilion before running for mayor, so I felt prepared for the endeavor.

The primary reason I decided to run for mayor was that people had asked me to. Before my election, many people were disenchanted with the mayor. They felt things needed to change and Vermilion needed help. After several people voiced to me they thought I would be the right person for the job and offered to help me with the campaign, I made the decision to run.

During my campaign, I used several different campaign techniques. I had booths at each of our city's two annual festivals. I did a couple drop mailings and distributed large and small yard signs. I also had inserts put in the local paper, and at the primary, I handed out forget-me-not seed packets. The method I felt was the most effective was going door-to-door to meet the voters. However, the biggest challenge to this method is being able to schedule enough time to reach people in the evenings when they were most likely to be home. I was forced to do some of my door-to-door visits during the day when it people were less likely to be available to talk.

I personally do not like negative campaigning, and I did not initiate it during my campaign. However, I did feel forced to address the many accusations my opponent made. I did not want the voters to think those accusations had any merit to them.

The best advice I could give someone interested in running for a local political office is to give it some serious thought before running. Campaigning requires time and energy. Even though I was surrounded by people willing to help, I had to do many things myself. The voters want to talk to the candidate, not the candidate's volunteers. They might call you at home, show up at your house, or stop you in the grocery store to discuss a political issue with you. A prospective candidate needs to be mentally prepared and willing to dedicate themselves to the job.

Political action committees

One of the most effective ways candidates can run negative campaigns while giving the appearance they were not involved with the ad's creation is through a political action committee (PAC). PACs are groups that are associated with either a political party or a specific issue with which a candidate stands for or is involved. The PAC is run outside the candidate's campaign, and the candidate does not pay the PAC for its work.

PACs generally gain their own financial backing through fundraisers and donors who support their issue. They run attack ads against the candidate who does not agree with their view or is in the other party. For example, in 2004, a group called Swift Boat Veterans for Truth ran ads blasting presidential candidate John Kerry for his depiction of swift boat sailors and service members during the Vietnam War. Fellow candidate and incumbent President George W. Bush was able to avoid any involvement in the row between the group and Kerry because the political group ran the ads, and they were not connected to Bush's campaign.

PAC use is not widely seen in local elections except perhaps in mayoral races in large cities because of the cost and hassle these committees incur. PACs can raise and spend as much money as some whole campaigns, so spending that amount of money on a local election would not get the kind of return that would justify the investment. PACs seek their own supporters and donations from individuals who support the idea or person they are promoting. For example, the Swift Boat Veterans for Truth were seeking to sway people toward voting for George W. Bush. They did this by appealing to veterans who might not appreciate Kerry's actions. Rather than directly advocating that people vote for Bush, they advocated that people should not vote for Kerry. Individuals donate money to PACs because they support the cause, which is the same reason people donate to candidates' campaigns or charitable organizations.

Other shady tactics

Candidates have other ways to run negative campaigns while steering clear of the blame. Candidates can leak information to the media that paints their opponent in a bad light and might not be accurate. News media are often eager to use tips they get about political candidates and campaigns to generate headlines.

Another way to participate in negative campaigning is through interest groups that carry out their own fundraisers to purchase ad time and run their own politically motivated commercials. Like a PAC, interest groups are not connected to a particular campaign but focus on an issue and back the candidate who supports their stance. Unlike PACs, which are created mostly for elections and then disbanded or dissolved after the election is over, interest groups are established organizations that will support a candidate or issue through the campaign and continue to lobby their issue once the candidate is elected. Interest groups are often well-funded organizations that are solely focused on promoting their issue and getting politicians to back their policy. They do not have the interest of the people in mind, which is something voters look for in a local candidate.

For a local candidate, being tied to an interest group might not be a good idea because local government needs to be responsive to the public because the public has easy access to local politicians. If you tie your campaign to an interest group, you could be viewed as putting the interests of that group ahead of the interest of the constituents. Although it is important to separate the campaign's motivations from the interest groups' motivations, interest groups can benefit a candidate. First, they represent voters who support the candidate. Second, they will use their own time and resources to promote the candidate to the voting public. Finally, interest groups might be willing to conduct fundraisers on the candidate's behalf or host political events for the candidate.

Why some candidates use these tactics

Politicians use negative campaigning because it has been long-standing in the history of political campaigns. Many feel it is just the way things are done. The first example of negative campaigning took place during the first contested presidential election between John Adams and Thomas Jefferson. Although neither candidate personally took jabs at the other, supporters on both sides made negative comments about the other candidate. The Jefferson campaign accused Adams of being a monarchical sympathizer who wanted to limit the freedoms of Americans, and the Adams camp leveled rumors that painted Jefferson as a French sympathizer and radical.

History has shown Adams, as president, did not install a monarchy, and Jefferson's radicalism never appeared during his two terms as president, yet the charges and slanders played a role in the campaign. Many presidential elections since this time have featured negative campaigning that called into question the character of the political opponents.

This is also the biggest reason negative campaigning has seeped into local elections. Presidential elections are the highest profile elections we have in the country. Presidential elections can draw anywhere from 65 to 70 percent of the voting population to the polls. Because voting is popular, the news media will cover nearly anything related to an election or a political candidate. This leads to the rapid spread of negative campaign messages.

Despite the fact negative campaigning can be difficult to avoid, local election campaigns can be run without its use. Although it is easy to make negative statements and reveal personal information about your opposition, it is just as easy to run a positive campaign. Each candidate can agree in advance to keep the election positive and focus on the needs of the community. Candidates have easy access to voters and can spread their message without taking shots at their opponent's character. In a local election, developing trust and communicating directly with voters to address their needs are better tactics.

NOT SLIPPING IN THE MUD

Campaigns can get personal when candidates do not censor the information they release to the public. Although not all candidates will be willing to respect their opposition's privacy, showing your own willingness to respect privacy might encourage that same respect in your opponent. Additionally, even if your opponent does decide to make the campaign personal, you can make the decision to keep your campaign professional. The following tips can help you keep the campaign professional:

- Make the decision to plan a positive campaign no matter how your opponent runs his or her campaign.

- Make a list of the information from your research of the opposition that applies to the campaign issues and another list of the information that does not apply.

- Approach your opponent at the start of the campaign to attempt a mutual agreement about which information is appropriate for the campaign.

- Be prepared with positive and appropriate responses to possible attacks.

☑ CHAPTER CHECKLIST

☐ Examine the information available to you about your opponent.

☐ Decide which information you plan to use in your campaign and which information you do not plan to make public.

☐ If you do plan to pursue negative campaigning, decide how and when you will release the possibly damaging information you are holding on to.

CHAPTER 10

Down to the Election Wire

· · · · · · · · · · · · · · · · · · · ·

As in any contest, what you do during the last moments of a campaign can be the most important. You worked hard to gather supporters and resources during the early months of your campaign, but it will have been for nothing if you cannot turn those efforts into votes on election day. Even if early polls show you are not in the lead, continue working toward your goal of winning the election.

What you do during the last two weeks before an election and even on election day itself can make a difference in who wins. The home stretch of any campaign will require effort on your part. It will be the busiest time for you. Be sure to set time aside for yourself and to spend with your family.

Two Weeks before the Election

Many undecided voters only begin paying attention to the messages of the candidates in the last two weeks of the election. Your staunchest supporters will have already made up their minds on who to vote for, so the voters who have not made a decisions yet will most likely give the election to one candidate or another.

The good news is that, by now, your message is finely tuned and tested. You also know it works because you have used it to draw in supporters already. One of the best ways to show undecided voters your message is one they should support is by hosting a rally during the last weeks of the election. Rallies are gatherings of your supporters, and the more the better. Rallies are also an opportunity to attract new voters. When individuals see a large group of people supporting one candidate, they tend to gravitate toward that candidate to learn more. Rallies are also a way to increase your name recognition. Hosting a rally during the final weeks of the campaign could attract the remaining swing voters who have yet to make a solid decision.

Rallies are used in all levels of government, but national levels offer the best examples, such as the party conventions before the presidential election and the election itself. In most cases, the party's nomination is set, and who will get the nomination to run for president is no real surprise. The convention, however, plays an important role as a rally. Televised, these conventions feature thousands of people cheering, waving flags, and wildly supporting their candidate and party. This is a campaign ploy to persuade more people to support their candidate. An undecided voter who watches this rally on the television might be drawn to an issue the rally is supporting. This same level of excitement can be duplicated at any level of government. Rallies can also be organized and conducted for relatively low cost.

But how do you use this campaign tactic in a local election, particularly when television stations might not cover your rally? You can use this to your benefit by making your rally as public as possible. A centralized public park in your city or town can be a good place to hold a rally. Because so many people are gathered in one location, others might go to the rally simply to see what is going on, which will get your name in the minds of more voters. Speeches are a huge part of any rally. When the nominee stands up to give his or her address, no new information is presented. Rehash what you have said before. This is not the time to bring in new ideas. This is the time to hammer home the key points of your message. The idea is to give people, and specifically undecided voters, a quick snapshot of what you stand for. The cheering crowd adds the exclamation point to your message. The last two weeks of your campaign are all about generating energy, and rallies are a way to accomplish that goal.

How to plan a political rally

Political rallies are a way to build excitement and gain support. Political rallies are especially popular among younger voters, such as college students. Rallies are most effective during the final weeks of the campaign. If the rally is too early in the campaign, the excitement it produces will have fizzled by the time voting day comes. A campaign team, a political party, or an independent group that supports the candidate can plan a political rally.

Do not plan too many rallies within a short period of time. Doing so will make supporters choose which rally to attend and result in lower attendance at each of the rallies. A rally with poor attendance will create the image that the candidate does not have a strong support base. Plan a handful of rallies the campaign committee is to host. When other groups offer to plan a rally on the candidate's behalf, space dates a couple of weeks apart.

Compile a list of campaign volunteers who are willing to work on the planning of a rally and at the actual rally. Volunteer activities will include setting up the rally location, cleaning up afterward, organizing the flow of events, and inviting people. One of the most important things volunteers can do is invite people to the rally and announce the rally throughout the community.

Have rally signs made. Rally signs should come in a variety of shapes and sizes, and they should all have the candidate's name on them. There should be smaller signs for people to hold and larger signs to hang up around the location of the rally. Post one sign on the front of the podium the speakers will be standing at and hang one large sign behind the podium. The two signs will be visible to any media cameras recording the event.

Make sure the location you choose for the rally is public and easily accessible to attendants and media personnel. The location should either have a stage or be large enough to set up a rented stage. The stage will allow the speakers to be higher than the crowd, which will make them more visible. Set up a working sound system for the speakers. Also set up tables for campaign literature, and station people to sign up new volunteers and accept donations. Campaign staff should also arrange security for the rally to ensure the safety of all those who attend.

Invite a wide variety of notable individuals to speak at the rally. This can include current or former politicians, prominent business leaders, local celebrities, or sports figures. Each speaker will only need to speak for a couple of minutes to endorse the candidate and excite the crowd. The candidate should be the last to speak at the rally. The candidate's job will be to thank the crowd for coming to the rally, reiterate the campaign message, and encourage everyone to go to the polls and vote on election day.

Get the media involved in the rally. To do this, send press releases to local media outlets, including newspapers, television stations, and local radio stations. A media presence at the rally will extend the excitement and show of support to those who were unable to attend the event. Involving the media will also increase the candidate's name recognition and help spread the candidate's message.

Finally, leading up to the rally, the most important thing the campaign staff and volunteers can do is advertise the event. Volunteers should hang fliers and posters around town to announce the rally. Advertise at campaign booths set up at local fairs or festivals. Everyone associated with the rally should verbally invite people to the rally.

On the day of the event, have a master of ceremonies (MC) introduce each speaker before they go on stage and thank each speaker as they leave the stage. The MC can also be in charge of inserting music into the rally between speeches, which helps aid in the excitement of the crowd and prevents awkward silences while someone is leaving or entering the stage area. Someone should also be given the task of calling local radio stations the day of the event in an attempt to make an announcement about the rally on air. Finally, at the end of the event, the crowd should be informed of the next major rally, fundraiser, or opportunity to get involved in the campaign.

Remember-to-vote campaigns

Another way to spread your message is through remember-to-vote or get-out-and-vote campaigns. These campaigns get your name to potential voters while reminding them an election is coming up. Many people do not vote, especially on the local level, simply because they did not know an election was being held. Reminding citizens they have the opportunity to vote is a good way to get them to the polls and get your name on their minds before they go. Offering free transportation to the polls is also a way to get people to the polls. Low voter turnout can be devastating to a well-planned campaign.

As part of this effort, candidates can help register potential voters. This effort can be as simple as providing registration cards at local fairs and festivals or as elaborate as hosting a register-to-vote event. This would be a special event planned with the goal of giving people the opportunity to attend and become a registered voter. This event, planned similarly to a fundraising event, can include food and entertainment and speakers encouraging people to vote. An ideal target audience for this type of event is high school seniors or recent graduates who are now old enough to vote but have not voted in the past. Helping these young voters get registered and providing them with information on where they should go to vote is a public relations move. It might also be the first experience a new voter has with a political candidate. New voters are also a source of potential volunteers.

Do not to tamper with the registration forms or try to control which party the voter registers with. Your job with this type of event is simply to give the public the opportunity to complete a registration form. You are doing citizens a public service and should be grateful they are participating no matter which party they register with. You should also check your local guidelines to find out whether hosting this type of event is acceptable as a candidate in the election. Also, in many areas, a voter must register a certain number of days before the actual election to be eligible to vote. Knowing this information can help you appropriately schedule your event.

One Week Before the Election

Many voters do not make their final decision about whom they plan to vote for until the last minute, so the weeks leading up to the election are often the most important. During the week before the election, you should send your final mailing if you are using direct mailings as part of your campaign. You should also have a final push in advertising if you are paying for newspaper, television, or radio advertisements.

Another way to reach voters during the week of the election is to have your supporters write letters to the editors of your local newspapers. Ask them to write letters describing why they support you and what you plan to do in office. You can even write a letter encouraging people to vote on election day. Once again, encouraging people to vote, regardless of who they vote for, is a good public relations move on your part.

If you still have not reached areas in your district during your door-to-door canvass, take time this week to visit those houses. Even canvassing during the day when people are less likely to be home will give you the opportunity to leave campaign literature at their door. It is important to continue your campaign up to election day. Use this last week before the election to do whatever you can to get your name and message out to potential voters.

The Day Before Elections

On the day before the election, you should make yourself accessible to the public. Hang out at the grocery store, library, coffee shop, or other busy public location. Be available to talk to people, answer questions, remind them about election day, and thank them for their support. Voters like having contact with candidates. Making yourself public will show you are accessible. Use this last day to talk to as many people as possible.

At the end of the day, take time to organize your thoughts and rest. Election day will likely be an anxious day, and you will have a lot to do. It is important to be prepared both physically and mentally. Have in mind what you want to say to your supporters and the public if you win and if you lose. Although getting the results might be an emotional moment for all candidates, it is important to remain professional and be prepared to make a statement about your win or loss.

Election Day

With all the hard work done, you have finally reached election day. However, this does not mean you can sit back and just watch the votes roll in. Election day is a busy day for candidates and another way to get your message out. The first thing any candidate should do on election day is vote. Beyond that, election day is a whirlwind of excitement and motion that ends with either a jubilant party or a congratulatory phone call to your opponent.

Some candidates choose to grant interviews to local news agencies, such as radio or television stations, on election day. In these interviews, you should thank your supporters for a hard-fought campaign, reaffirm your message, and thank the voters for going out to the polls to support you. These last-minute interviews will improve your image whether you win or lose. It is important to maintain your image even if you lose in case you decide to run in a future election.

Campaigning at the polls is restricted in most states to reduce tampering and voter intimidation. However, it is not completely eliminated in all states, so look into your local laws about campaigning at the polls. If it is allowed, you can station yourself and volunteers at the most popular polling center and distribute fliers or brochures. You can also help arrange transportation for individuals who need help getting to the polls on election day. Many campaigns also station volunteers at important locations throughout the city, such as major street intersections, to hold campaign signs and wave at passersby. This reminds the public it is election day and could help get better voter turnout.

In addition to all that, it is customary for a candidate to hold a celebration for all those who have worked hard to get you elected. These parties are a way to rally your supporters and either head into office on a high note or thank everyone for their effort. The location of the party could be campaign headquarters or another predetermined location. As the polls close, campaign workers and volunteers will gather at the party location and wait for election results. The candidate will also be at the party location waiting for the results. The campaign party does not have to be elaborate. There should be food or snacks, drinks, and in case you win, champagne and balloons or confetti to aid in the celebration.

Results, Polls, and Your Opponent

A long wait for results often characterize smaller races. However, once they do begin to come in, the results are often clear in a matter of minutes because only one or two wards or districts need to be counted to determine the winner.

For larger races, such as county elections or elections in large cities, watching results come in can be an unnerving task. As results come in from different districts and areas, the number of votes for you and your opponent can vary wildly depending on where your pockets of support were. Don't put too much emphasis on early results, and wait for the majority of votes to be counted. On election nights, most local news stations have a continually updated report on election results. Candidates might choose to watch the news as the results come or monitor the results online through a news media website.

Some candidates find exit polls important. Pollsters either a candidate or a media outlet hires wait outside voting stations to ask voters who they voted for. Voters do not have to answer the question pollsters pose unless they want to, and there is no way to tell whether they are answering truthfully. Therefore, you might not get an accurate feel for the way the public is voting. A good example of this was in the 2000 election between George W. Bush and Al Gore. During that election, many news networks called Florida for Gore based on exit polling data and counties that got their final counts in early. It turned out the polling data was off, and these news networks were later forced to remove Florida as a win for Gore and put it back in play. The state eventually went to Bush — along with the presidency.

Once the results are in and a winner is certain, it is the losing candidate's responsibility to call the winning candidate and congratulate him or her on a well-run campaign and the victory.

Transitioning from Candidate to Elected Official

The election results are in, and you have won. What should you do next? During the months following a campaign, it is the duty of the elected official and the outgoing official to collaborate on a successful power transition.

This will involve learning the ropes. There are also classes and training seminars to help newly elected officials. Newly elected politicians have the tasks of learning their new job, fulfilling their campaign promises, and staying focused on the big picture. Everything a candidate does while in office can affect future campaigns. Balance current needs with future aspirations.

☑ CHAPTER CHECKLIST

- ❏ Plan and carry out at least one rally during the last two weeks.
- ❏ Participate in remember-to-vote efforts and events.
- ❏ Brainstorm any last-minute efforts to get your name out to the voters.
- ❏ Make sure you have completed everything you planned to leading up to the election.
- ❏ Make sure you vote.
- ❏ Host your campaign party.

CHAPTER 11

You've Won! Now What?

After a long and difficult campaign, winning feels pretty good. You should take some time to enjoy it. Earning a victory in an election is no small task. You have shown the voters you are trustworthy, and your message has resonated with the public. However, the relief of a campaign ending is soon replaced with the work required to transition from a candidate to an elected official. All members must know the rules and regulations that run government bodies. Also, members of a government body must be well acquainted with all the issues facing that position, not just the ones that garnered headlines during the campaign.

The first thing you should do after winning an election is thank everyone. You need to publicly thank your staff, volunteers, donors, and all the people who voted for you. This is the appropriate thing to do, and not thanking everyone can start your term off on a bad foot with the people you are representing. An election night party is a common way to thank all the volunteers and staff for their hard work and dedication.

Learning the Job

As with any new job, a training period exists during which all public officials must learn the do's and don'ts of serving in public office. Luckily for newly elected candidates, most states and local governments offer classes and training seminars for newcomers. These classes and seminars focus on the laws and the rules that govern public meetings. Other methods of learning the job include speaking with other members of the local government with whom you will be working, talking to individuals who previously held the position, and talking to any seasoned politicians who possess knowledge of your job.

All public meetings have certain rules that must be abided by. Many government bodies will use Roberts Rules of Order to govern their meetings. These rules lay the groundwork for who can speak during public meetings, how members will be recognized, which issues can be discussed, and in which order things will be discussed. New candidates must learn the importance of public notices for meetings, the decorum that must be displayed to demonstrate an orderly government body, and certain rules the government body might have in addition to Roberts Rules of Order. Newly elected officials must also meet with the incumbents and other elected officials to learn the issues the municipality faces.

The newly elected official must also focus on gaining all the information he or she needs to fulfill the promises he or she made during the election. Fulfilling election promises says a lot about the trustworthiness of the candidate. The bureaucracy might also hold training sessions because these workers are active in the day-to-day operations of the government and might be responsible for training newly elected officials.

Reinforcing Your Message

After you are elected, you should meet with your supporters and reinforce the message of your campaign. Let them know what you have been learning in your new position, and offer some of the ways you will be able to reach your goals.

Once you have won one election, the campaign for the next election begins. Making your supporters an important part of your transition into office will show you are now willing to work to make sure their wishes are represented in the government.

Including your supporters in your transition can also garner you more support in the community. Many voters are apathetic and simply assume once someone is elected, he or she will be unable to do what was promised during the election or will not interact with the public in general. Interacting with your supporters after you are elected could show those who did not vote for you previously you are a person of your word who will work for their needs. This type of interaction and reconnection with the public is a tactic an increasing number of politicians have used.

The Next Campaign

Keep in mind once the election is over, the next campaign begins. Unless you are in an office that has term limits, every politician is also a candidate for his or her job. Keep your campaign message active and in the minds of voters. If you are successful in fulfilling your campaign promises, your previous message will benefit you in future elections. For some high-profile positions in bigger municipalities, this means hiring campaign volunteers as part of your staff once you are elected. By doing this, the people who helped you get into office are there to help you while you are in office and eventually when the next election rolls around.

For most local elected positions, however, there is no position in which to hire people. To keep that structure alive, keep the key contributors to your campaign in the loop. Let them know their continued participation in government is essential for you to achieve the goals you set during your campaign. Keep them well-informed on the issues, and continue to keep your name on the minds of the voters by remaining active in your new position, being available for interviews with news personnel, and raising points or asking questions during discussions.

Also, keep your social networking, blogs, and websites active. Just as they were when you were running for office, these methods are a fast, cheap, and efficient way of communicating with the public. A quick post on Facebook that reads, "Town meeting tonight. Going to discuss water rates. Need to find a way to keep them low," can show voters you are still looking out for them, are in touch with the issues, and want to communicate with the people who elected you into office.

This also lets voters know what is going on in local government. Many feel government is a massive entity operating in secrecy. Reaching out to the public and inviting them in will create goodwill. And because you are in office already, you gain the advantage of being an incumbent. The hardest thing to do is unseat a popular incumbent, which is right where you want to be.

You've Lost! Now What?

The first thing you want to do after losing an election is congratulate your opponent. Be a gracious loser even if you are overwhelmed with disappointment. You do not need to issue a public statement; you can simply call your opponent and congratulate him or her personally. After you have done this, you need to thank all the people who supported you throughout the campaign. This includes your supporters, members of your team, your family, your volunteers, and your donors. Although you might feel pressured to make promises about future elections, it is best to leave it open at this point.

Give yourself some time to emotionally get over the loss, and then begin organizing your thoughts for the future. You still care about the area you were hoping to represent, so get involved with various committees and community groups. This will allow you to be active in your community regardless of whether you run again in the future. Carefully consider what is best for the people within the district.

Finally, take a careful look at the entire election. Examine your strengths and the strengths of your opponent. Was the election lost because of differences in campaigning or qualifications? If the other candidate was simply better qualified for the job, you should accept this and work to gain more experience to help you in the future. If the campaign was lost because of campaign strategies, you should stay involved and consider using a different campaign manager during the next election.

☑ CHAPTER CHECKLIST

If you won:

☐ Congratulate your opponent on a well-fought campaign.

☐ Enjoy the celebration party.

☐ Thank all your volunteers and supporters.

☐ Learn how to do your new job.

☐ Work toward fulfilling your campaign promises.

☐ Make notes on things that will benefit you in future campaigns.

If you lost

☐ Congratulate your opponent.

☐ Thank all your volunteers and supporters.

☐ Evaluate your campaign, and make notes for future campaigns.

Conclusion

C ampaigning can be a stressful process for candidates and their families. Keep the focus of the campaign on why you wanted to run in the first place. You are running for a political office because you wanted to get involved with your community and help make things better. You have examined the issues, and you know the specific changes you would like to see made. Do not let the stress of the campaign or the rivalry with your opponent lead you down a path you did not intend to travel. Avoid being caught up in name-calling or mudslinging. Additionally, do not make promises or statements as brash responses to your opponents' attacks. Doing so could cause the downfall of your campaign.

Choose a Campaign Strategy that Works for You

• •

Although the point of hiring professionals is to have people available to offer advice and make recommendations on actions, this is your campaign. Avoid strategies or fundraising events you do not feel adequately represent you or you are not comfortable with.

Likewise, do not feel forced into debates or arguments you are not prepared for. Emotions can cause you to say things you would not have said if you had been thinking clearly. Everything you say during a campaign can be interpreted in different ways. Be prepared with statements and responses to general questions that have your focus and platform in mind. Do not allow yourself to be lured into an argument with the other candidates, opposing supporters, or journalists.

Finally, journalists are not your friends. Some journalists will spin a conversation or comment any way they need to get an exciting story out of it. Do not be tricked into having a casual conversation with someone who happens to work for a newspaper. Nothing is ever off the record when you are running for a political office.

Enjoy Yourself

This might seem like odd advice after hearing how stressful political campaigns are, but running for a political office and being intimately involved with a political campaign are exciting experiences not everyone gets to have. You will have the opportunity to attend events you would not normally attend, meet new and interesting people every day, and inspire others to follow their dreams. Embrace this time in your life, and enjoy it for what it is. If you win the election, you can go on to enjoy life in a political office. If you do not win the election, you can savor the experience and focus on your future decisions.

Chapter Checklists

· ·

T

he following checklists are the same checklists that appear at the end of each chapter throughout the book. They have been included here as a resource.

Chapter 1 Checklist:

❑ Find out the type of local government under which your area operates.

❑ Get a list of the elected positions from the clerk's office.

❑ Research each position to determine the qualifications needed to be successful in the position.

❑ Disregard any position for which you are not qualified.

❑ Research the responsibilities of the remaining positions to determine whether they fit your qualifications.

❑ Talk to people who formerly held the position to determine what time commitment is involved.

❑ Based on this information, decide whether you want to run for a particular political office.

Chapter 2 Checklist:

❑ Answer the questions posed in the first part of this chapter.

❑ Write down your political goals.

❑ Chose the elected position you want to run for.

❑ Collect information from the clerk's office about voter activity in past elections for this position.

❑ Decide which political affiliation you want to run under, if any.

❑ Disaffiliate from your current political party if you need to.

❑ Attend government meetings and passively collect information about issues within the community.

❑ Make a list of the issues and goals in your community.

❑ Compare the list of community issues with your political goals.

❑ Look into who is currently holding the position.

❑ Find out whether that person is eligible for re-election.

❑ Find out how many times the incumbent has been elected to that position.

❑ Find out whether the incumbent is popular with citizens. All this information will be necessary as you assemble your campaign plan. *The campaign plan will be explained fully in Chapter 4.*

Chapter 3 Checklist:

- ❑ Hire a campaign manager.
- ❑ With the campaign manager, decide which other professionals will be needed based on the size of your campaign.
- ❑ Hire the remaining needed professionals.
- ❑ Have a meeting with everyone to create team cohesion and make sure everyone understands you and your message.
- ❑ Create volunteer recruiting cards.
- ❑ Begin recruiting volunteers for the campaign.

Chapter 4 Checklist:

- ❑ Collect copies of all the election laws that apply to the position for which you intend to run.
- ❑ Pick up all needed forms from the clerk's office, including the nomination petitions and monetary disclosure forms.
- ❑ Collect nomination signatures.
- ❑ Read and fill out monetary disclosure forms.
- ❑ Meet with your core team and create your campaign plan.
- ❑ Have your volunteer coordinator begin organizing and recruiting volunteers.
- ❑ Create the design for your signs.
- ❑ Create your slogan if you chose to have one.
- ❑ Have professional photos taken to use during your campaign.

Chapter 5 Checklist:

- ❏ Investigate election laws regarding budgets and donations.
- ❏ Create a list of expenses, and gather estimates of cost.
- ❏ Create a list of revenue sources.
- ❏ Develop a fundraising plan based on the amount of money needed.
- ❏ Initiate your fundraising plan, and follow through until the needed funds are raised.
- ❏ Investigate the availability of public funds.
- ❏ Send thank-you cards to all donors.

Chapter 6 Checklist:

- ❏ Choose campaigning methods.
- ❏ Buy advertising space in newspapers and time on the radio and television.
- ❏ Organize town hall meetings or local debates with your opponent.
- ❏ Organize and attend several meet-and-greets.
- ❏ Distribute yard signs to supporters.
- ❏ Approach local businesses to gain support.
- ❏ Seek out valuable endorsements.

Chapter 7 Checklist:

- ❏ Choose the social networking websites you are most comfortable using.
- ❏ Set up a campaign website with your information, experience, and message along with photos and a calendar of events.
- ❏ Look into a web design company if necessary.

❑ Create a blog and link it to your website for online visitors to easily access.

❑ Create links from your website to your social networking pages.

❑ Update regularly. It does not need to be daily, but your supporters want to hear from you.

Chapter 8 Checklist:

❑ Conduct research into your opponent.

❑ Organize information into a format you can easily read and examine.

❑ Make an extensive list of your opponent's strengths and weaknesses.

❑ Include all pertinent information about your opponent in your campaign plan.

❑ Consider which information can be used to boost your campaign and which should be held back.

❑ If some of the information is questionable, do more research to verify the information is correct.

Chapter 9 Checklist:

❑ Examine the information available to you about your opponent.

❑ Decide which information you plan to use in your campaign and which information you do not plan to make public.

❑ If you do plan to pursue negative campaigning, decide how and when you will release the possibly damaging information you are holding on to.

Chapter 10 Checklist:

❏ Plan and carry out at least one rally during the last two weeks.

❏ Participate in remember-to-vote efforts and events.

❏ Brainstorm any last-minute efforts to get your name out to the voters.

❏ Make sure you have completed everything you planned to leading up to the election.

❏ Make sure you vote.

❏ Host your campaign party.

Chapter 11 Checklist:

If you won:

❏ Congratulate your opponent on a well-fought campaign.

❏ Enjoy the celebration party.

❏ Thank all your volunteers and supporters.

❏ Learn how to do your new job.

❏ Work toward fulfilling your campaign promises.

❏ Make notes on things that will benefit you in future campaigns.

If you lost:

❏ Congratulate your opponent.

❏ Thank all your volunteers and supporters.

❏ Evaluate your campaign, and make notes for future campaigns.

Creating a Campaign Plan

··

The following sections describe the items you should include in your campaign plan. *This information was discussed in Chapter 4.*

Section 1: Background Research

- List potential opposition, including the incumbent and possible challengers.
- Provide a detailed list of responsibilities of the position you are running for.
- Include copies of all applicable election laws in your district.
- Determine how many voters are in your district.
- Determine what percentage of registered voters in your district actually vote.
- Determine how many votes you will need to win the election.

- Include copies of nomination forms.
- Determine how many signatures are required to secure a nomination.
- Include contribution limits.
- Retrieve copies of the monetary disclosure forms.
- Include a list of important deadlines for the nomination forms and disclosure forms.

Section 2: You and Your Opponent

- Write a detailed description of yourself, including your childhood, education, and work history.
- Describe why you want to run for office.
- Describe the roots of your interest in politics.
- Describe your opponent in detail.
- Read through all the information discovered during your research of your opponent, and compile it in an easy-to-read format.

Section 3: Goals

- Describe your personal goals, such as whether you are hoping to only run for a local office or whether you are hoping to work your way up in politics.
- Describe your goals for the position you are running for.
- Describe why you are running for this office.
- Describe what you are hoping to accomplish.
- Write down all your goals even if you are not sure yet what you will realistically be able to accomplish. Goals can always be re-evaluated later in the campaign.

Section 4: Targeting

- Describe the voters in your district.
- Determine where the swing voters are in your district.
- Describe the demographics of the swing voters.
- Describe how you plan to reach the swing voters.
- Include maps of the entire voting district.
- Highlight different areas on the map to show where swing voters and support voters are primarily located.

Section 5: Key Issues

- Describe in a few sentences each of the key issues in your area.
- Describe where voters stand on these issues.
- Describe which political actions have been made in regards to these issues.
- Determine whether voters are generally happy or dissatisfied with the actions of the incumbents.
- Determine whether you can capitalize on any new issues.

Section 6: Your Position on Key Issues

- For each key issue identified in the previous section, write an official statement for your position on the issue. Create these statements with the help of your campaign team. These statements will be the ones released to the media, and you will commit them to memory and be able to reiterate their content when questioned.
- List any action you have taken to demonstrate your position on the key issues.

Section 7: Campaign Message

- Write your official campaign message. Base this on the information gathered in sections 3 and 6 of the campaign plan. The campaign message will be the basis for the items in Section 8.

Section 8: Slogan, Logo, and Campaign Literature

- Based on your campaign message, create a catchy campaign slogan.
- Create your official campaign logo, which should include your name.
- Have professional pictures taken, and include proofs of each picture in this section.
- Decide on the types of campaign literature you plan to use.
- With the help of your campaign team, design your campaign literature.
- Get samples of the possible campaign literature from a print shop, and include the samples in this section.
- Compare the samples to decide which campaign literature you plan to use, and get estimates of printing costs.

Section 9: Campaign Strategies

- Make a complete list of all possible campaign strategies you are willing to use.
- Get a list of public events you can participate in during the course of the campaign.
- Get cost estimates for campaign strategies.
- Determine which campaign strategies have been successful in the past or for other candidates.

- Decide which strategies are you comfortable using.

Section 10: Campaign Schedule

- Include a monthly, weekly, and daily planner in your campaign plan.
- Record all large events on the monthly calendar.
- Create a campaigning schedule starting with election day and working backward to the start of the campaign period.
- Once the campaign schedule is complete, add everything to your monthly, weekly, and daily planner.
- Leave room in the schedule for events that arise during the campaign.
- Include possible dates for fundraising events and rallies in the schedule.

Section 11: Budget

- Make a list of all possible expenses.
- Get cost estimates for all possible expenses.
- Make a list of income sources.
- Compile a list of potential donors.
- Look for other sources of funding.
- Plan the types of fundraisers you are going to hold and the amount of money you realistically think you will bring in at each fundraiser.
- Based on your estimated income, decide how you will spend the money and where you can cut costs.

Section 12: Team Members

- Include a directory with all the contact information for each of the team members.

Examples of Political Speeches

George W. Bush
Sixth State of the Union Address
January 31, 2006

Thank you all. Mr. Speaker, Vice President Cheney, members of Congress, members of the Supreme Court and diplomatic corps, distinguished guests, and fellow citizens:

Today our nation lost a beloved, graceful, courageous woman who called America to its founding ideals and carried on a noble dream. Tonight we are comforted by the hope of a glad reunion with the husband who was taken so long ago, and we are grateful for the good life of Coretta Scott King.

Every time I'm invited to this rostrum, I'm humbled by the privilege, and mindful of the history we've seen together. We have gathered under this Capitol dome in moments of national mourning and national achievement. We have served America through one of the most consequential periods of our history — and it has been my honor to serve with you.

In a system of two parties, two chambers, and two elected branches, there will always be differences and debate. But even tough debates can be conducted in a civil tone, and our differences cannot be allowed to harden into anger. To confront the great issues before us, we must act in a spirit of goodwill and respect for one another — and I will do my part. Tonight the state of our Union is strong — and together we will make it stronger.

In this decisive year, you and I will make choices that determine both the future and the character of our country. We will choose to act confidently in pursuing the enemies of freedom — or retreat from our duties in the hope of an easier life. We will choose to build our prosperity by leading the world economy — or shut ourselves off from trade and opportunity. In a complex and challenging time, the road of isolationism and protectionism may seem broad and inviting — yet it ends in danger and decline. The only way to protect our people, the only way to secure the peace, the only way to control our destiny is by our leadership — so the United States of America will continue to lead.

Abroad, our nation is committed to an historic, long-term goal — we seek the end of tyranny in our world. Some dismiss that goal as misguided idealism. In reality, the future security of America depends on it. On September 11th, 2001, we found that problems originating in a failed and oppressive state 7,000 miles away could bring murder and destruction to our country. Dictatorships shelter terrorists, and feed resentment and radicalism, and seek weapons of mass destruction. Democracies replace resentment with hope, respect the rights of their citizens and their neighbors, and join the fight against terror. Every step toward freedom in the world makes our country safer — so we will act boldly in freedom's cause.

Far from being a hopeless dream, the advance of freedom is the great story of our time. In 1945, there were about two dozen lonely democracies in the world. Today, there are 122. And we're writing a new chapter in the story of self-government — with women lining up to vote in Afghanistan, and millions of Iraqis marking their liberty with purple ink, and men and women from Lebanon to Egypt debating the rights of individuals and the necessity of freedom. At the start of 2006, more than half the people of our world live in democratic nations. And we do not forget the other half — in places like Syria and Burma, Zimbabwe, North Korea, and Iran — because the demands of justice, and the peace of this world, require their freedom, as well.

No one can deny the success of freedom, but some men rage and fight against it. And one of the main sources of reaction and opposition is radical Islam — the perversion by a few of a noble faith into an ideology of terror and death. Terrorists like bin Laden are serious about mass murder — and all of us must take their declared intentions seriously. They seek to impose a heartless system of totalitarian control throughout the Middle East, and arm themselves with weapons of mass murder.

Their aim is to seize power in Iraq, and use it as a safe haven to launch attacks against America and the world. Lacking the military strength to challenge us directly, the terrorists have chosen the weapon of fear. When they murder children at a school in Beslan, or blow up commuters in London, or behead a bound captive, the terrorists hope these horrors will break our will, allowing the violent to inherit the Earth. But they have miscalculated: We love our freedom, and we will fight to keep it.

In a time of testing, we cannot find security by abandoning our commitments and retreating within our borders. If we were to leave these vicious attackers alone, they would not leave us alone. They would simply move the battlefield to our own shores. There is no peace in retreat. And there is no honor in retreat. By allowing radical Islam to work its will — by leaving an assaulted world to fend for itself — we would signal to all that we no longer believe in our own ideals, or even in our own courage. But our enemies and our friends can be certain: The United States will not retreat from the world, and we will never surrender to evil.

America rejects the false comfort of isolationism. We are the nation that saved liberty in

Europe, and liberated death camps, and helped raise up democracies, and faced down an evil empire. Once again, we accept the call of history to deliver the oppressed and move this world toward peace. We remain on the offensive against terror networks. We have killed or captured many of their leaders — and for the others, their day will come.

We remain on the offensive in Afghanistan, where a fine President and a National Assembly are fighting terror while building the institutions of a new democracy. We're on the offensive in Iraq, with a clear plan for victory. First, we're helping Iraqis build an inclusive government, so that old resentments will be eased and the insurgency will be marginalized.

Second, we're continuing reconstruction efforts, and helping the Iraqi government to fight corruption and build a modern economy, so all Iraqis can experience the benefits of freedom. And, third, we're striking terrorist targets while we train Iraqi forces that are increasingly capable of defeating the enemy. Iraqis are showing their courage every day, and we are proud to be their allies in the cause of freedom.

Our work in Iraq is difficult because our enemy is brutal. But that brutality has not stopped the dramatic progress of a new democracy. In less than three years, the nation has gone from dictatorship to liberation, to sovereignty, to a constitution, to national elections. At the same time, our coalition has been relentless in shutting off terrorist infiltration, clearing out insurgent strongholds, and turning over territory to Iraqi security forces. I am confident in our plan for victory; I am confident in the will of the Iraqi people; I am confident in the skill and spirit of our military. Fellow citizens, we are in this fight to win, and we are winning. The road of victory is the road that will take our troops home. As we make progress on the ground, and Iraqi forces increasingly take the lead, we should be able to further decrease our troop levels — but those decisions will be made by our military commanders, not by politicians in Washington, D.C.

Our coalition has learned from our experience in Iraq. We've adjusted our military tactics and changed our approach to reconstruction. Along the way, we have benefitted from responsible criticism and counsel offered by members of Congress of both parties. In the coming year, I will continue to reach out and seek your good advice. Yet, there is a difference between responsible criticism that aims for success, and defeatism that refuses to acknowledge anything but failure. Hindsight alone is not wisdom, and second-guessing is not a strategy.

With so much in the balance, those of us in public office have a duty to speak with candor. A sudden withdrawal of our forces from Iraq would abandon our Iraqi allies to death and prison, would put men like bin Laden and Zarqawi in charge of a strategic country, and show that a pledge from America means little. Members of Congress, however we feel about the decisions and debates of the past, our nation has only one option: We must keep our word, defeat our enemies, and stand behind the American military in this vital mission.

Our men and women in uniform are making sacrifices — and showing a sense of duty stronger than all fear. They know what it's like to fight house to house in a maze of streets, to wear heavy gear in the desert heat, to see a comrade killed by a roadside bomb. And those who know the costs also know the stakes. Marine Staff Sergeant Dan Clay was killed last month fighting in Fallujah. He left behind a letter to his family, but his words could just as well be addressed to every American. Here is what Dan wrote: "I know what honor is. It has been an honor to protect and serve all of you. I faced death with the secure knowledge that you would not have to... Never falter! Don't hesitate to honor and support those of us who have the honor of protecting that which is worth protecting."

Staff Sergeant Dan Clay's wife, Lisa, and his mom and dad, Sara Jo and Bud, are with us this evening. Welcome. Our nation is grateful to the fallen, who live in the memory of our country. We're grateful to all who volunteer to wear our nation's uniform — and as we honor our brave troops, let us never forget the sacrifices of America's military families.

Our offensive against terror involves more than military action. Ultimately, the only way to defeat the terrorists is to defeat their dark vision of hatred and fear by offering the hopeful alternative of political freedom and peaceful change. So the United States of America supports democratic reform across the broader Middle East. Elections are vital, but they are only the beginning. Raising up a democracy requires the rule of law, and protection of minorities, and strong, accountable institutions that last longer than a single vote.

The great people of Egypt have voted in a multi-party presidential election — and now their government should open paths of peaceful opposition that will reduce the appeal of radicalism. The Palestinian people have voted in elections. And now the leaders of Hamas must recognize Israel, disarm, reject terrorism, and work for lasting peace. Saudi Arabia has taken the first steps of reform — now it can offer its people a better future by pressing forward with those efforts. Democracies in the Middle East will not look like our own, because they will reflect the traditions of their own citizens. Yet liberty is the future of every nation in the Middle East, because liberty is the right and hope of all humanity.

The same is true of Iran, a nation now held hostage by a small clerical elite that is isolating and repressing its people. The regime in that country sponsors terrorists in the Palestinian territories and in Lebanon — and that must come to an end. The Iranian government is defying the world with its nuclear ambitions, and the nations of the world must not permit the Iranian regime to gain nuclear weapons. America will continue to rally the world to confront these threats.

Tonight, let me speak directly to the citizens of Iran: America respects you, and we respect your country. We respect your right to choose your own future and win your own freedom. And our nation hopes one day to be the closest of friends with a free and democratic Iran. To overcome dangers in our world, we must also take the offensive by encouraging economic progress, and fighting disease, and spreading hope in hopeless lands. Isolationism would not only tie our hands in fighting enemies, it would keep us from helping our friends in desperate need. We show compassion abroad because Americans believe in the God-given dignity and worth of a villager with HIV/AIDS, or an infant with malaria, or a refugee fleeing genocide, or a young girl sold into slavery. We also show compassion abroad because regions overwhelmed by poverty, corruption, and despair are sources of terrorism, and organized crime, and human trafficking, and the drug trade.

In recent years, you and I have taken unprecedented action to fight AIDS and malaria, expand the education of girls, and reward developing nations that are moving forward with economic and political reform. For people everywhere, the United States is a partner for a better life. Short-changing these efforts would increase the suffering and chaos of our world, undercut our long-term security, and dull the conscience of our country. I urge members of Congress to serve the interests of America by showing the compassion of America.

Our country must also remain on the offensive against terrorism here at home. The enemy has not lost the desire or capability to attack us. Fortunately, this nation has superb professionals in law enforcement, intelligence, the military, and homeland security. These men and women are dedicating their lives, protecting us all, and they deserve our support and our thanks. They also deserve the same tools they already use to fight drug trafficking and organized crime — so I ask you to reauthorize the Patriot Act.

It is said that prior to the attacks of September 11th, our government failed to connect the dots of the conspiracy. We now know that two of the hijackers in the United States placed telephone calls to al Qaeda operatives overseas. But we did not know about their plans until it was too late. So to prevent another attack — based on authority given to me by the Constitution and by statute — I have authorized a terrorist surveillance program to aggressively pursue the international communications of suspected al Qaeda operatives and affiliates to and from America. Previous Presidents have used the same constitutional authority I have, and federal courts have approved the use of that authority. Appropriate members of Congress have been kept informed. The terrorist surveillance program has helped prevent terrorist attacks. It remains essential to the security of America. If there are people inside our country who are talking with al Qaeda, we want to know about it, because we will not sit back and wait to be hit again.

In all these areas — from the disruption of terror networks, to victory in Iraq, to the spread of freedom and hope in troubled regions — we need the support of our friends and allies. To draw that support, we must always be clear in our principles and willing to act. The only alternative to American leadership is a dramatically more dangerous and anxious world. Yet we also choose to lead because it is a privilege to serve the values that gave us birth. American leaders — from Roosevelt to Truman to Kennedy to Reagan — rejected isolation and retreat, because they knew that America is always more secure when freedom is on the march. Our own generation is in a long war against a determined enemy — a war that will be fought by Presidents of both parties, who will need steady bipartisan support from the Congress. And tonight I ask for yours. Together, let us protect our country, support the men and women who defend us, and lead this world toward freedom.

Here at home, America also has a great opportunity: We will build the prosperity of our country by strengthening our economic leadership in the world. Our economy is healthy and vigorous, and growing faster than other major industrialized nations. In the last two-and-a-half years, America has created 4.6 million new jobs — more than Japan and the European Union combined. Even in the face of higher energy prices and natural disasters, the American people have turned in an economic performance that is the envy of the world.

The American economy is preeminent, but we cannot afford to be complacent. In a dynamic world economy, we are seeing new competitors, like China and India, and this creates uncertainty, which makes it easier to feed people's fears. So we're seeing some old temptations return. Protectionists want to escape competition, pretending that we can keep our high standard of living while walling off our economy. Others say that the government needs to take a larger role in directing the economy, centralizing more power in Washington and increasing taxes. We hear claims that immigrants are somehow bad for the economy — even though this economy could not function without them. All these are forms of economic retreat, and they lead in the same direction — toward a stagnant and second-rate economy. Tonight I will set out a better path: an agenda for a nation that competes with confidence; an agenda that will raise standards of living and generate new jobs. Americans should not fear our economic future, because we intend to shape it.

Keeping America competitive begins with keeping our economy growing. And our economy grows when Americans have more of their own money to spend, save, and invest. In the last five years, the tax relief you passed has left $880 billion in the hands of American workers, investors, small businesses, and families — and they have used it to help produce more than four years of uninterrupted economic growth. Yet the tax relief is set to expire in the next few years. If we do nothing, American families will face a massive tax increase they do not expect and will not welcome.

Because America needs more than a temporary expansion, we need more than temporary tax relief. I urge the Congress to act responsibly, and make the tax cuts permanent.

Keeping America competitive requires us to be good stewards of tax dollars. Every year of my presidency, we've reduced the growth of non-security discretionary spending, and last year you passed bills that cut this spending. This year my budget will cut it again, and reduce or eliminate more than 140 programs that are performing poorly or not fulfilling essential priorities. By passing these reforms, we will save the American taxpayer another $14 billion next year, and stay on track to cut the deficit in half by 2009. I am pleased that members of Congress are working on earmark reform, because the federal budget has too many special interest projects. And we can tackle this problem together, if you pass the line-item veto.

We must also confront the larger challenge of mandatory spending, or entitlements. This year, the first of about 78 million baby boomers turn 60, including two of my Dad's favorite people — me and President Clinton. This milestone is more than a personal crisis — it is a national challenge. The retirement of the baby boom generation will put unprecedented strains on the federal government. By 2030, spending for Social Security, Medicare and Medicaid alone will be almost 60 percent of the entire federal budget. And that will present future Congresses with impossible choices — staggering tax increases, immense deficits, or deep cuts in every category of spending.

Congress did not act last year on my proposal to save social security, yet the rising cost of entitlements is a problem that is not going away. And every year we fail to act, the situation gets worse.

So tonight, I ask you to join me in creating a commission to examine the full impact of baby boom retirements on Social Security, Medicare, and Medicaid. This commission should include members of Congress of both parties, and offer bipartisan solutions.

We need to put aside partisan politics and work together and get this problem solved.

Keeping America competitive requires us to open more markets for all that Americans make and grow. One out of every five factory jobs in America is related to global trade, and we want people everywhere to buy American. With open markets and a level playing field, no one can out-produce or out-compete the American worker.

Keeping America competitive requires an immigration system that upholds our laws, reflects our values, and serves the interests of our economy. Our nation needs orderly and secure borders. To meet this goal, we must have stronger immigration enforcement and border protection. And we must have a rational, humane guest worker program that rejects amnesty, allows temporary jobs for people who seek them legally, and reduces smuggling and crime at the border.

Keeping America competitive requires affordable health care. Our government has a responsibility to provide health care for the poor and the elderly, and we are meeting that responsibility. For all Americans, we must confront the rising cost of care, strengthen the doctor-patient relationship, and help people afford the insurance coverage they need.

We will make wider use of electronic records and other health information technology, to help control costs and reduce dangerous medical errors. We will strengthen health savings accounts — making sure individuals and small business employees can buy insurance with the same advantages that people working for big businesses now get. We will do more to make this coverage portable, so workers can switch jobs without having to worry about losing their health insurance. And because lawsuits are driving many good doctors out of practice — leaving women in nearly 1,500 American counties without a single OB/GYN — I ask the Congress to pass medical liability reform this year.

Keeping America competitive requires affordable energy. And here we have a serious problem: America is addicted to oil, which is often imported from unstable parts of the world. The best way to break this addiction is through technology. Since 2001, we have spent nearly $10 billion to develop cleaner, cheaper, and more reliable alternative energy sources — and we are on the threshold of incredible advances.

So tonight, I announce the Advanced Energy Initiative — a 22-percent increase in clean-energy research — at the Department of Energy, to push for breakthroughs in two vital areas. To change how we power our homes and offices, we will invest more in zero-emission coal-fired plants, revolutionary solar and wind technologies, and clean, safe nuclear energy. We must also change how we power our automobiles. We will increase our research in better batteries for hybrid and electric cars, and in pollution-free cars that run on hydrogen. We'll also fund additional research in cutting-edge methods of producing ethanol, not just from corn, but from wood chips and stalks, or switch grass. Our goal is to make this new kind of ethanol practical and competitive within six years.

Breakthroughs on this and other new technologies will help us reach another great goal: to replace more than 75 percent of our oil imports from the Middle East by 2025. By applying the talent and technology of America, this country can dramatically improve our environment, move beyond a petroleum-based economy, and make our dependence on Middle Eastern oil a thing of the past.

And to keep America competitive, one commitment is necessary above all: We must continue to lead the world in human talent and creativity. Our greatest advantage in the world has always been our educated, hardworking, ambitious people — and we're going to keep that edge. Tonight I announce an American Competitiveness Initiative, to encourage innovation throughout our economy, and to give our nation's children a firm grounding in math and science.

First, I propose to double the federal commitment to the most critical basic research programs in the physical sciences over the next ten years. This funding will support the work of America's most creative minds as they explore promising areas such as nanotechnology, supercomputing, and alternative energy sources.

Second, I propose to make permanent the research and development tax credit to encourage bolder private-sector initiatives in technology. With more research in both the public and private sectors, we will improve our quality of life — and ensure that America will lead the world in opportunity and innovation for decades to come.

Third, we need to encourage children to take more math and science, and to make sure those courses are rigorous enough to compete with other nations. We've made a good start in the early grades with the No Child Left Behind Act, which is raising standards and lifting test scores across our country. Tonight I propose to train 70,000 high school teachers to lead advanced placement courses in math and science, bring 30,000 math and science professionals to teach in classrooms, and give early help to students who struggle with math, so they have a better chance at good, high-wage jobs. If we ensure that America's children succeed in life, they will ensure that America succeeds in the world.

Preparing our nation to compete in the world is a goal that all of us can share. I urge you to support the American Competitiveness Initiative, and together we will show the world what the American people can achieve.

America is a great force for freedom and prosperity. Yet our greatness is not measured in power or luxuries, but by who we are and how we treat one another. So we strive to be a

compassionate, decent, hopeful society. In recent years, America has become a more hopeful nation. Violent crime rates have fallen to their lowest levels since the 1970s. Welfare cases have dropped by more than half over the past decade. Drug use among youth is down 19 percent since 2001. There are fewer abortions in America than at any point in the last three decades, and the number of children born to teenage mothers has been falling for a dozen years in a row.

These gains are evidence of a quiet transformation — a revolution of conscience, in which a rising generation is finding that a life of personal responsibility is a life of fulfillment.

Government has played a role. Wise policies, such as welfare reform and drug education and support for abstinence and adoption have made a difference in the character of our country. And everyone here tonight, Democrat and Republican, has a right to be proud of this record. Yet many Americans, especially parents, still have deep concerns about the direction of our culture, and the health of our most basic institutions. They're concerned about unethical conduct by public officials, and discouraged by activist courts that try to redefine marriage. They worry about children in our society who need direction and love, and about fellow citizens still displaced by natural disaster, and about suffering caused by treatable diseases. As we look at these challenges, we must never give in to the belief that America is in decline, or that our culture is doomed to unravel. The American people know better than that. We have proven the pessimists wrong before — and we will do it again.

A hopeful society depends on courts that deliver equal justice under the law. The Supreme Court now has two superb new members — new members on its bench: Chief Justice John Roberts and Justice Sam Alito. I thank the Senate for confirming both of them. I will continue to nominate men and women who understand that judges must be servants of the law, and not legislate from the bench.

Today marks the official retirement of a very special American. For 24 years of faithful service to our nation, the United States is grateful to Justice Sandra Day O'Connor.

A hopeful society has institutions of science and medicine that do not cut ethical corners, and that recognize the matchless value of every life. Tonight I ask you to pass legislation to prohibit the most egregious abuses of medical research: human cloning in all its forms, creating or implanting embryos for experiments, creating human-animal hybrids, and buying, selling, or patenting human embryos. Human life is a gift from our Creator — and that gift should never be discarded, devalued or put up for sale.

A hopeful society expects elected officials to uphold the public trust. Honorable people in

both parties are working on reforms to strengthen the ethical standards of Washington — I support your efforts. Each of us has made a pledge to be worthy of public responsibility — and that is a pledge we must never forget, never dismiss, and never betray.

As we renew the promise of our institutions, let us also show the character of America in our compassion and care for one another.

A hopeful society gives special attention to children who lack direction and love. Through the Helping America's Youth Initiative, we are encouraging caring adults to get involved in the life of a child — and this good work is being led by our First Lady, Laura Bush. This year we will add resources to encourage young people to stay in school, so more of America's youth can raise their sights and achieve their dreams.

A hopeful society comes to the aid of fellow citizens in times of suffering and emergency — and stays at it until they're back on their feet. So far the federal government has committed $85 billion to the people of the Gulf Coast and New Orleans. We're removing debris and repairing highways and rebuilding stronger levees. We're providing business loans and housing assistance.

Yet as we meet these immediate needs, we must also address deeper challenges that existed before the storm arrived.

In New Orleans and in other places, many of our fellow citizens have felt excluded from the promise of our country. The answer is not only temporary relief, but schools that teach every child, and job skills that bring upward mobility, and more opportunities to own a home and start a business. As we recover from a disaster, let us also work for the day when all Americans are protected by justice, equal in hope, and rich in opportunity.

A hopeful society acts boldly to fight diseases like HIV/AIDS, which can be prevented, and treated, and defeated. More than a million Americans live with HIV, and half of all AIDS cases occur among African Americans. I ask Congress to reform and reauthorize the Ryan White Act, and provide new funding to states, so we end the waiting lists for AIDS medicines in America. We will also lead a nationwide effort, working closely with African American churches and faith-based groups, to deliver rapid HIV tests to millions, end the stigma of AIDS, and come closer to the day when there are no new infections in America.

Fellow citizens, we've been called to leadership in a period of consequence. We've entered a great ideological conflict we did nothing to invite. We see great changes in science and commerce that will influence all our lives. Sometimes it can seem that history is turning in a wide arc, toward an unknown shore. Yet the destination of history is determined by human action, and every great movement of history comes to a point of choosing.

Lincoln could have accepted peace at the cost of disunity and continued slavery. Martin Luther King could have stopped at Birmingham or at Selma, and achieved only half a victory over segregation. The United States could have accepted the permanent division of Europe, and been complicit in the oppression of others. Today, having come far in our own historical journey, we must decide: Will we turn back, or finish well?

Before history is written down in books, it is written in courage. Like Americans before us, we will show that courage and we will finish well. We will lead freedom's advance. We will compete and excel in the global economy. We will renew the defining moral commitments of this land. And so we move forward — optimistic about our country, faithful to its cause, and confident of the victories to come.

May God bless America.

William J. Clinton
First Inaugural Address
January 20, 1993

My fellow citizens:

Today we celebrate the mystery of American renewal. This ceremony is held in the depth of winter. But, by the words we speak and the faces we show the world, we force the spring. A spring reborn in the world's oldest democracy, that brings forth the vision and courage to reinvent America.

When our founders boldly declared America's independence to the world and our purposes to the Almighty, they knew that America, to endure, would have to change. Not change for change's sake, but change to preserve America's ideals; life, liberty, the pursuit of happiness. Though we march to the music of our time, our mission is timeless. Each generation of Americans must define what it means to be an American.

On behalf of our nation, I salute my predecessor, President Bush, for his half-century of service to America. And I thank the millions of men and women whose steadfastness and sacrifice triumphed over Depression, fascism and Communism.

Today, a generation raised in the shadows of the Cold War assumes new responsibilities in a world warmed by the sunshine of freedom but threatened still by ancient hatreds and new plagues.

Raised in unrivaled prosperity, we inherit an economy that is still the world's strongest, but is weakened by business failures, stagnant wages, increasing inequality, and deep divisions among our people.

When George Washington first took the oath I have just sworn to uphold, news traveled slowly across the land by horseback and across the ocean by boat. Now, the sights and sounds of this ceremony are broadcast instantaneously to billions around the world.

Communications and commerce are global; investment is mobile; technology is almost magical; and ambition for a better life is now universal. We earn our livelihood in peaceful competition with people all across the earth.

Profound and powerful forces are shaking and remaking our world, and the urgent question of our time is whether we can make change our friend and not our enemy.

This new world has already enriched the lives of millions of Americans who are able to compete and win in it. But when most people are working harder for less; when others cannot work at all; when the cost of health care devastates families and threatens to bankrupt many of our enterprises, great and small; when fear of crime robs law-abiding citizens of their freedom; and when millions of poor children cannot even imagine the lives we are calling them to lead, we have not made change our friend.

We know we have to face hard truths and take strong steps. But we have not done so. Instead, we have drifted, and that drifting has eroded our resources, fractured our economy, and shaken our confidence.

Though our challenges are fearsome, so are our strengths. And Americans have ever been a restless, questing, hopeful people. We must bring to our task today the vision and will of those who came before us.

From our revolution, the Civil War, to the Great Depression to the civil rights movement, our people have always mustered the determination to construct from these crises the pillars of our history.

Thomas Jefferson believed that to preserve the very foundations of our nation, we would need dramatic change from time to time. Well, my fellow citizens, this is our time. Let us embrace it.

Our democracy must be not only the envy of the world but the engine of our own renewal. There is nothing wrong with America that cannot be cured by what is right with America.

And so today, we pledge an end to the era of deadlock and drift; a new season of American renewal has begun. To renew America, we must be bold.

We must do what no generation has had to do before. We must invest more in our own people, in their jobs, in their future, and at the same time cut our massive debt. And we must do so in a world in which we must compete for every opportunity. It will not be easy; it will require sacrifice. But it can be done, and done fairly, not choosing sacrifice for its own sake, but for our own sake. We must provide for our nation the way a family provides for its children.

Our Founders saw themselves in the light of posterity. We can do no less. Anyone who has ever watched a child's eyes wander into sleep knows what posterity is. Posterity is the world to come; the world for whom we hold our ideals, from whom we have borrowed our planet, and to whom we bear sacred responsibility. We must do what America does best: offer more opportunity to all and demand responsibility from all.

It is time to break the bad habit of expecting something for nothing, from our government or from each other. Let us all take more responsibility, not only for ourselves and our families but for our communities and our country. To renew America, we must revitalize our democracy.

This beautiful capital, like every capital since the dawn of civilization, is often a place of intrigue and calculation. Powerful people maneuver for position and worry endlessly about who is in and who is out, who is up and who is down, forgetting those people whose toil and sweat sends us here and pays our way.

Americans deserve better, and in this city today, there are people who want to do better. And so I say to all of us here, let us resolve to reform our politics, so that power and privilege no longer shout down the voice of the people. Let us put aside personal advantage so that we can feel the pain and see the promise of America. Let us resolve to make our government a place for what Franklin Roosevelt called "bold, persistent experimentation," a government for our tomorrows, not our yesterdays. Let us give this capital back to the people to whom it belongs.

To renew America, we must meet challenges abroad as well at home. There is no longer division between what is foreign and what is domestic; the world economy, the world environment, the world AIDS crisis, the world arms race; they affect us all.

Today, as an old order passes, the new world is more free but less stable. Communism's collapse has called forth old animosities and new dangers. Clearly America must continue to lead the world we did so much to make.

While America rebuilds at home, we will not shrink from the challenges, nor fail to seize the opportunities, of this new world. Together with our friends and allies, we will work to shape change, lest it engulf us.

When our vital interests are challenged, or the will and conscience of the international community is defied, we will act; with peaceful diplomacy whenever possible, with force when necessary. The brave Americans serving our nation today in the Persian Gulf, in Somalia, and wherever else they stand are testament to our resolve.

But our greatest strength is the power of our ideas, which are still new in many lands. Across the world, we see them embraced, and we rejoice. Our hopes, our hearts, our hands, are with those on every continent who are building democracy and freedom. Their cause is America's cause.

The American people have summoned the change we celebrate today. You have raised your voices in an unmistakable chorus. You have cast your votes in historic numbers. And you have changed the face of Congress, the presidency and the political process itself. Yes, you, my fellow Americans have forced the spring. Now, we must do the work the season demands.

To that work I now turn, with all the authority of my office. I ask the Congress to join with me. But no president, no Congress, no government, can undertake this mission alone. My fellow Americans, you, too, must play your part in our renewal. I challenge a new generation of young Americans to a season of service; to act on your idealism by helping troubled children, keeping company with those in need, reconnecting our torn communities. There is so much to be done; enough indeed for millions of others who are still young in spirit to give of themselves in service, too.

In serving, we recognize a simple but powerful truth, we need each other. And we must care for one another. Today, we do more than celebrate America; we rededicate ourselves to the very idea of America.

An idea born in revolution and renewed through two centuries of challenge. An idea tempered by the knowledge that, but for fate we, the fortunate and the unfortunate, might have been each other. An idea ennobled by the faith that our nation can summon from its myriad diversity the deepest measure of unity. An idea infused with the conviction that America's long heroic journey must go forever upward.

And so, my fellow Americans, at the edge of the 21st century, let us begin with energy and hope, with faith and discipline, and let us work until our work is done. The scripture says, "And let us not be weary in well-doing, for in due season, we shall reap, if we faint not."

From this joyful mountaintop of celebration, we hear a call to service in the valley. We have heard the trumpets. We have changed the guard. And now, each in our way, and with God's help, we must answer the call.

Thank you, and God bless you all.

Glossary

Absentee ballot: The ballot used by voters who are unable to go to a polling station on election day.

Ballot: The actual form used to record an individual's vote.

Blog: An online forum that allows candidates to address the public through written posts.

Board of elections: The official board set up to oversee the elections in each area.

Campaign schedule: The calendar of events the candidate arranges for his or her campaign, which will include debates, fundraisers, public appearances, and door-to-door canvassing.

Campaign literature: The printed material the candidate has made to distribute to potential voters. Campaign literature might include fliers, pamphlets, and posters.

Campaign manager: A hired professional who will

help the candidate plan his or her campaign strategy and oversee the day-to-day functions of the campaign.

Campaign message: The official statement the candidate makes. It includes what they want to accomplish if elected.

Campaign plan: A detailed manual of campaign plans. The campaign plan will include the goals, objectives, budget, campaign strategies, fundraising efforts, donor lists, and research on the opposition.

Campaign trail: This refers to the time the candidate spends meeting with voters and actively campaigning.

Candidate: The individual running for a political office.

Canvassing: Covering an area to either meet with voters or to distribute campaign literature.

Canvassing involves going to individual houses.

Debate: A public event that allows multiple candidates to present their positions on specific issues. Debates also provide candidates with the opportunity to confront each other in a professional manner.

Direct voter contact: Campaign activities that bring the candidate to the voters. This can include door-to-door canvassing or participating in public events.

Disclosure forms: Paperwork candidates are required to complete when they decide to run for office that provide information about their income, financial status, and business associations.

District: The geographic area containing the voters that are eligible to vote for a specific position.

District research: Information gathered to determine the needs and issues within a specific district and information about the voters' voting habits.

Earned media: When a candidate is featured in the news because of things he or she is doing or saying. This is media attention the candidate does not pay money to receive.

Endorsements: Written or verbal shows of support from influential people, political parties, organizations, or businesses.

Exit polling: Voters are questioned about who they voted for as they leave the polling stations.

Incumbent: A candidate running for a position they currently hold.

Internet campaigning: This includes any campaign strategies conducted online, including websites, blogs, social networking, and e-mails.

Name recognition: When voters know who a candidate is based on his or her name. Candidates with strong name recognition are more likely to be remembered at the polls.

Nomination petition: The official document needed to pursue candidacy.

Nomination period: The period of time individuals are eligible to enter a political race and be listed on the ballot.

Nonpartisan: A position that is not associated with a specific political party.

Opposition research: Gathering information about the individual a candidate will be running against.

Political party: A party such as Republican, Democrat, or Independent party.

Polling station: The physical location where individuals will go to vote.

Press release: A specific type of written statement used to provide information to the media.

Slogan: A catchy phrase used to sum up a candidate's campaign message.

Social networking: Websites such as Facebook, MySpace, and Twitter used to spread information and gain name recognition.

Swing precinct: A precinct within a voting district that does not have a solid voting history with a specific political party.

Swing voters: Individual voters who do not always vote for a specific political party.

Targeting: Researching an area to determine who the swing voters are.

Town hall meeting: A type of debate that is more casual and allows voters to ask the candidates questions.

Volunteer: Individuals who do work for a campaign without being paid because they want that candidate to win the election.

Volunteer coordinator: An individual assigned the task of recruiting, training, and organizing the volunteers during a political campaign.

Bibliography

Fusco, P. (2010). *Running: How to Design and Execute a Winning Political Campaign*. Schenectady, NY: PI&MVR Writings Co.

Grey, L. (2007). *How to Win a Local Election*.
Lanham, Maryland: M. Evans.

Halbfinger, David. (2010). "Rough Start for Big Name in Conn. Senate Race." The New York Times. Retrieved from: **www. nytimes.com/2010/04/15/nyregion/15blumenthal.html**.

U.S. Census Bureau. (2005). "Individual State Descriptions: 2002" U.S. Department of Commerce: Economics and Statistics Administration. Volume 1, Number 2.

Litwack, Maury. (2010). "Dr. King got it wrong – the metric of a successful political rally." The Daily Caller. Retrieved from: **http://dailycaller.com/2010/10/04/the-metric-of-a-successful-political-rally**.

Mangu-Ward, K. (2010). "8 percent of Americans Want to See Congress Reelected. 90 Percent of Congressmen will Be Reelected." Reason: Hit & Run. Retrieved from Reason: **http://reason.com/blog/2010/02/12/8-percent-of-americans-want-to**.

McNamara, M. (2008). *The Political Campaign Desk Reference: A guide for campaign managers and candidates running for elected office*. Denver, Colorado: Outskirts Press, Inc.

Personke, S. (2003). "How to Successfully Plan a Gala Fundraising Event for a Library." Retrieved from: **www.infotoday.com/mls/mar03/howto.shtml**.

"Ron Paul Courageously Speaks the Truth." (2007). YouTube. Retrieved from: **www.youtube.com/watch?v=G7d_e9lrcZ8**.

Shaw, C. (2010). *The Campaign Manager: Running and Winning Local Elections*. Philadelphia, PA: Westview Press.

Sweet, Lynn. (2008). "Warren Buffett to headline $28,500-per-person 'private dinner' for Obama at finance chair Penny Pritzker home; senior advisor Valerie Jarrett a host." Chicago Sun-Times. Retrieved from Sun-Times: **http://blogs.suntimes.com/sweet/2008/06/warren_buffett_to_headline_285.html**.

Thomas, R. (2008). *How to Run for Local Office: A Complete Guide for Winning a Local Election*. Alger, Michigan: R&T Enterprise Inc.

Wolfe, Lahle. (2010). "Twitter Statistics: How Many People Use Twitter?" Women in Business. Retrieved from About.com: **http://womeninbusiness.about.com/od/twittertips/a/twitter-statistics.htm**.

Author Biography

Having studied political science as an undergraduate student at Bowling Green State University, Melanie Williamson has had a long-standing interest in politics and local government. Writing this book has given her the opportunity to further her knowledge on the day-to-day realities of running for a political office and to talk to a number of local politicians, campaign volunteers, and campaign managers. Her hope is that this book will help encourage others to get involved in the politics of their local community.

Index